Hereward Kirby Cockin

Gentleman Dick

And Other Poems

Hereward Kirby Cockin

Gentleman Dick
And Other Poems

ISBN/EAN: 9783337005429

Printed in Europe, USA, Canada, Australia, Japan

Cover: Foto ©Thomas Meinert / pixelio.de

More available books at **www.hansebooks.com**

GENTLEMAN DICK
O' THE GREYS

And Other Poems

BY

HEREWARD K. COCKIN.

.

Reader! an' should this effort serve to while
One weary moment, or provoke a smile,
The Author's heart will thank the cudgell'd brains
That flung the mirth and pathos of these strains :
Born they of quiet hours from month to year—
The laurel wreath beyond, the cypress near,
While struggling on through true and false report,
Cheer'd by success, by sad reverses taught ;
(Reverse, well used, is victory in disguise,
Bereft of it true effort wanes and dies.
Undue success is worse than dire defeat,
Capua was more disastrous than retreat,
For he, who by the Capuan ease undone,
Dishonoured, forfeits that which Cannæ won,
And greater he, who oft defeated, still
Fights on, untamed and undismayed, until
His steady courage bears his foeman down, ·
And wrests from him the victor's laurel crown.)

TORONTO :
C. BLACKETT ROBINSON

hundred and eighty-nine by HEREWARD K. COCKIN, in the office of the Minister of Agriculture.

TO

PROFESSOR GOLDWIN SMITH, LL.D., D.C.L.

THESE POEMS ARE SINCERELY INSCRIBED

AS AN IMPERIAL UNIONIST'S HONEST TRIBUTE OF RESPECT FOR AN EMINENT

AND FEARLESS PUBLICIST,

WHOSE KINDLINESS OF HEART, HIGH SENSE OF PERSONAL HONOUR

AND SINGLENESS OF PURPOSE, COMBINED WITH GREAT INTELLECTUAL GIFTS,

HAVE SECURED FOR HIM THE RESPECT AND ADMIRATION

OF BOTH CONTINENTS.

THE AUTHOR.

TORONTO, FEB., 1889.

	PAGE
Gentleman Dick o' the Greys	9
Parson Oldboy's Reverie	11
Lundfren's Vigil	13
The Old Church Must Go	17
Judas Iscariot	18
St. Hilda's Bells	19
To a Maple Leaf	20
Wharfedale	21
Lying Epitaphs	22
At Christmas-Tide	25
New Year's Eve	26
A Graveyard Idyll	27
"It Might Have Been"	29
Jesmonde Dene	30
Public Funerals	30
Dulce Domum	32
Tutor Non Ultor (1879)	34
The Man in the Park	35
Pomp De Scallawag; His Temptation and Fall	36
At the Vicarage Gate	39
Nothing Like Leather	40
The Happy Family	40
The Philosophy of the Clubs	47
In Memoriam: Dean Grasett	48
Dr. Tanner's Fast	49
From Gloom to Light	50
At the Trocadero	51
Sonnet to a Mule	52
How the Children Saved Naumburg	53
His Artist-Soul Returned	56
Scampkowski	57
The Death of Burnaby	58
The Vale of Lune	59
The Lord Mayor of York and his Brother Ned	61
Gethsemane	66

CONTENTS.

	PAGE
CHELLOW DENE	67
GUILIA'S PRAYER	68
THE MISSIONARY SHIP	68
LENTEN-TIDE	79
BELAY! BELAY THERE!	70
EXACTLY SO	70
OUR LITTLE DICK	71
THE VETERAN'S TALE	72
AT EVENTIDE	73
FAREWELL	74
ANGEL EUSTACE	75
VIOLET	75
BABY CLARENCE	76
ETHEL	77
TO A FRIEND	77
HEATON RISE	78
THE SIGHING OF THE FIRS	79
LITTLE GRETCHEN	80
THE RED HAND OF O'NEIL	81
EPITAPH ON AN EARLY SETTLER	84
THE TRAMP	86
TORONTO'S GLORIOUS DEAD	88
THESE DEGENERATE MODERN DAYS	89
THE DEATH BED OF LOUIS XI.	91
JACK TARTAR	94
THE OLD COACHING INN	98
THE PIC-NIC BOY	99
OLD PUFF	100
THE COUNTY STEEPLECHASE	102
BEREAVED	106
KILLED IN THE STRAIGHT	107
HIS NAME WAS BILL	107
ISAIAH BROWN	109
IN THE WARD OF ST. JOHN THE DIVINE	111
THE CYCLONE	113
THE DENTIST'S CHAIR	114
VANITY FAIR	115
"NINETY-EIGHT"	116

GENTLEMAN DICK O' THE GREYS,

AND OTHER POEMS.

GENTLEMAN DICK O' THE GREYS.

WE were chums, Dick and I, in the old college days,
 Came to grief on the " Oaks " and enlisted—the Greys.
Ne'er a braver than Dick ever sabre blade drew,
From his plume to his spurs he was leal and true,
And his bright, handsome features and devil care ways
Won the soubriquet, " Gentleman Dick o' the Greys."

Yet he fretted and chafed at our barrack-room life,
And he longed—how he longed! for the maddening strife;
How he sighed to forget all our " feather bed " calm,
In the wild, dashing charge, in the midnight alarm,
For he breathed but to tread in the footsteps of fame,
Which for him, gallant heart! was the pathway of shame.

Accurs'd be the hour when Bulstroder Hayes
Exchanged from the " Line " to our troop in " The Greys ";
Oh! the woe of a life 'neath a martinet's frown;
'Twas a story oft known in a garrison town,
When recruit and scarr'd veteran were under the rule
Of a tyrant from India or a youngster from school.

Hayes showed the " black heart " in a thousand of ways,
Ay, he made life a hell to the men of " The Greys,"
Till one day in the stables our captain, our foe,
Insulted poor Dick, and Dick answered—a blow ;
But the wrath that felled Hayes to the ground with a crash
Doomed " Gentleman Dick o' the Greys " to the lash.

Six squadrons, four deep on three sides of a square,
With the officers, doctor and " triangle " there,
And I, his old friend, saw him led to his shame—
To the infamy cast on a once honoured name—
Saw the drummer's dread thongs and the flesh torn—ah ! well !
From the young heart they crushed rose a demon of hell.

When the roll-call was answered one morn, all alone
He had fled where the brand of his shame was unknown ;
And the months came and went, then a rumour of war
Flung a sinister gloom on the fair lands afar ;
And we heard on parade, with an answering roar,
That the Greys had the route for the Crimean shore.

· · · · · · · ·

Down the valley their grey-coated infantry stepped,
In a whirlwind of fury their batteries swept,
But the Greys led the charge in the bright morning light,
With the French on our left and the Sixth on our right ;
And, swift as the bolt from the cloud lightning-riven,
The Muscovite flank on the centre was driven.

But, ere we could re-form our grape shatter'd ranks,
The Vladimir regiment burst on our flanks,
And 'twas hack, cut and slash—little parrying there—
If the Russians were devils what demons we were !
Right nobly our handful disputed the field,
For a Briton can die ! tho' he never can yield !

Three Russians beset me; at last I fought free,
Made much of my charger, and turned, God! to see
A Vladimir horseman charge Bulstroder Hayes,
And, 'midst the infuriate yells of the Greys,
Deliver cut six—and Hayes dropped from his horse,
And his curse-writhen lips were the lips of a corse.

Too late for his life—that had gasped its last breath—
But in time, by the Gods! to avenge him in death;
One prick of the spurs in the flanks of the grey,
Three bounds, and I held the fierce Russian at bay,
And crash! as their trumpeter sounded "the wheel,
From his skull to his teeth I had crimsoned the steel.

As the sabre-cleft helmet discovered his face,
As he fell from his charger in death, I had space
For a glance—oh! my God! at those wild staring eyes,
For one look at those features upturned to the skies,
And I reeled in the saddle, my brain all ablaze,
For the dead man was "Gentleman Dick o' the Greys"

―――

PARSON OLDBOY'S REVERIE.

IN my quiet country parsonage I sit amongst my books,
  And I hear the pigeons cooing and the cawing of the rooks,
As all tenderly the gloaming veils the sunset's parting glow,
And from hidden crypts of memory rise the forms of long ago.
Some still walk this vale of sadness, most have sought that dis-
    tant bourne,
Whence whose mystic lights and shadows mortal never may
    return.
Ah! in fancy I behold them, comrades of each passing joy,
In the dear old happy school days—days when I was yet a boy.

There was Jones, that knock-kneed youngster, yea, methinks I
see him now,
With his face all pale and ghastly at the mention of a row,
Yet he, *tempora mutantur*, far beyond those classic halls,
In the service of his country's Queen has dodged the cannon-
balls;
And so valorously he dodged 'em too, that fickle Mistress Fame,
And Her Majesty—God bless her!—tacked a " V. C." to his
name.
Absent are those erstwhile knee-bags, *vice* Jones' gay sabretache,
And his face is well-nigh hidden by a fierce dragoon moustache.

Oh! that "wet-bob," Swipes secundus! don't I see his frenzied
gait
As he guys those wretched "pair oars," as he chaffs the college
"eight"?
Often, oh, how often! after smoking surreptitious pipes
I have sought the arm of pale and penitential Robert Swipes.
What a soul he had for apples—"orchards" was his *nightly*
prayer,
And my mind's eye views the owner *mourning* for what was'nt
there;
But old Swipes is now my bishop, portly he in lawn and gown,
And the quidnuncs say his mitre crowns the driest Bob in town.

Curly-headed Oppidan! a lover he of boyish sports,
Often have I, out of pity, written Oppy's longs and shorts.
But, O tempora! O mores! Oppidan, with austere rule,
Birches human longs and shorts now in a country grammar
school.
Swishing minor, wretched youngster, was my fag in those blest
days;
How I used to whack and cuff him for his most uncleanly ways!
And I wish I'd whacked him ofter, for that snivelling little brute
Since those days has given judgment 'gainst me in a Chancery
suit.

Damesboy (he whose family crest is—well their crest Je ne sais
quoi—
But at any rate their motto is without a doubt " Bonne Foi,")
Lives a life of ease and pleasure, quite the opposite of slow.
(Will he ever send that fifty which he borrowed years ago ?)
Kingsclere, noble, handsome fellow, kindly heart and open hand!
Died a broken-hearted exile in the German Fatherland;
And the Baden townsfolk whisper how by his own hand he fell,
After losing fame and fortune at their whilom gambling-hell.

In my quiet country parsonage I sit amongst my books;
Silent now the dovecote's murmur, still'd the clamour of the
rooks;
Faded now the last beam's gilding, and the darkness settles fast;
Back! into your crypts, ye spectres! Vanish, phantoms of the
past.
For your train of byegone schoolmates fills me with a tender pain,
And your—but I hear a knocking, "Come in! Candles! Thank
you, Jean,
Nothing more except my hassock and, Jean, when you go down
stairs,
Place these letters in the bag, and bid the household come to
prayers."

LUNDFREN'S VIGIL.

Near the altar, in death, a young student lay sleeping,
    And the incense of flowers rose faint on the air,
As the gloaming of even came silently creeping,
    And enswathed in its shadows the dead, lying there.

Ah! ineffably sweet was the life of that sleeper,
    Though unknown to us all but one short year ago;
How we loved him—dear exile from shores where the reaper
    Blends his song with the echoes from San Angelo.

In the chancel we laid him, our custom in Sweden,
  And bedecked him with flowers, more exquisite far
Than the roses which bloom in that garden of Eden,
  From whose thousandfold fragrance springs India's attar.

In the bowl and the wine-cup we pledged our deep sorrow,
  As we gathered at night in Carl Weisselgren's room,
And we lovingly spake of the one, whom the morrow
  Would behold as he passed from the church to the tomb.

But the saddest of all was a pale-featured student,
  On whose shoulders, in curls, fell the long flaxen hair;
All impulsive was Lundfren, and, oftimes imprudent,
  Yet the soul of affection and honour dwelt there.

As in accents all broken by passionate weeping,
  Whilst the pathos of sorrow bedew'd his young face,
" Oh, Da Conti," he murmured, " I would I were sleeping
  In the Valley of Shadows, in thine honoured place.

" In the solemn death-watch, of the love that I bear thee,
  Ah! how earnest, indeed, was my heart-stricken prayer,
I entreated of heaven, in mercy, to spare thee,
  E'en tho' I, even I, should be sacrificed there."

" ' Ach in Schlingel! ' he cries like a weak-minded maiden,"
  Spake the harsh voice of one, as he entered the room,
" Not a heart ever beat, sirs, howe'er friendship laden,
  Would surrender one throb for the sepulchre's gloom."

With a frown, each one turned to confront the intruder,
  Fellow-student was he, yet not one of our band,
'Twas Von Bartel, a German, in bearing far ruder
  Than the boar of the woods in his own native land.

" Is there one of you all, tho' thus sighing and moaning,
   Who, to prove that affection is stronger than dread,
Ere the echoes of midnight have ceased their intoning,
   Dare imprint but one kiss on the lips of the dead?"

" Is there one? Ay, there's Lundfren, thou cynical scoffer,
   On whose forehead would mantle the hot blush of shame;
Was there one, save thyself, but would willingly proffer
   The oblation of self in affection's sweet name.

" When the dank dews of midnight are softly descending,
   Ere the blush of the Orient each mountain crest tips,
By the corpse of Da Conti my form will be bending,
   As I press the cold features of Death with my lips."

   .   .   .   .   .   .

Hark! The midnight booms out. On the face of him sleeping
   At the Altar of Death, is a dim halo shed,
By the candle that stands, like a sentinel, keeping
   Watch and ward, through the night, by the side of the dead.

In the shadowy aisles, 'neath the carved stones are sleeping
   The Lion of the North, and his queen, Elenore,
And (sad emblems of Sweden's long vigil of weeping)
   The heroes who bled in the Thirty Years' War.

From the gloom of the nave glides a figure, advancing,
   With the chill wave of fear on his brow and his heart;
God! how keenly that start and his timorous glancing
   Mark the soul that is stricken by horror's fell dart!

All alone near the dead, and with footsteps that falter,
   Whilst the gloom of the shadows their grim terrors lend,
By an effort he reaches the foot of the altar,
   And there gazes on him that in life was his friend.

With a gasp of repugnance, he bends low and stooping,
  Leaves a kiss on the lips and the cold ashen cheek,
As a hand all unseen grasps his mantle, and drooping,
  Riddarholmen* re-echoes his blood-curdling shriek.

For a moment he writhes in the throes of convulsion,
  Oh, the agonized wail of that sad parting moan,
As the soul from the body, in sudden expulsion,
  Wings its flight in dismay to the regions unknown.

And the maidens who gathered in awe-stricken wonder,
  By the bright flashing sunlight of morning-tide, said
'Twas the pangs of despair snapped his heart-strings asunder,
  And he cared not for life, since Da Conti was dead.

No, alas! it was terror. When swiftly uprising
  From the lips of Da Conti, the long trestle rod
Caught his gown, and it seemed to his heart's agonizing,
  That the pressure, above, was the hand of his God.

And the granite stemm'd winds that from Mälar came sweeping,
  Breathe a sad lullaby, where the pine branches wave,
In the Acre of God, o'er two student forms sleeping,
  Who, together in life, share in death the same grave.

But forever are silent the tones of their laughter,
  Till Eternity dawns, and all Time is no more,
When the loud blast shall summon the solemn hereafter,
  And the nations are met on the far away shore.

---

* The Westminster Abbey of Sweden, at Stockholm.

THE OLD CHURCH MUST GO.

(Dedicated to the numerous down town churches which have been abandoned).

EVER more shall I stand in yon dim shadow'd aisle,
　Where the voices, now hush'd, fill'd with rapture my heart;
Oh ! 'twas humble, I know, yet that time-honoured pile
　Can emotion awake, and the burning tear start.
Nor pillar of Corinth, nor white of Carrara
　Lent their charms to the scene where bright angels have trod ;
They, whose vision was clearer, whose pathway was nearer
　From the byways of earth to the mansions of God.

All around it now gather the gloom and the shadows,
　And the Babel of Dross rears its columns on high,
Where the echoes once gave to the fair upland meadows,
　The lowing of kine and the whip-poor-will's cry.
Gone ! gone ! the old friends, yet, methinks, once again
　There come to mine ears, through the dark city's gloom,
Loved accents of those, on whose cold lips have lain
　The silence of death, and the hush of the tomb.

Old church ! thou art doom'd ! all thine honour undone—
　The storm-rack has pass'd, and thy travail is o'er ;
Rend, O lever ! to base from the battlement stone
　For the hearts that have known it, shall know it no more.
How the fashion has changed ; statelier piles must be rear'd
　Nigh the mansion of wealth in some well favour'd spot ;
The old race has gone whom those walls have endeared,
　And the halo of mem'ry encircles them not.

Hark ! the legions of darkness have gather'd in hate :
　The garrison sleeps, while the foe presses on,
Soon the Fathers in Israel shall learn—ah ! too late !
　When the watch tower's deserted—the stronghold is won.

But the old church must go! " That sweet story of old,"
And the songs of old Zion are heard no more there ;
For each lover of lust, and the Mammon of gold,
Hath his seat on the altar once hallow'd by Prayer.

JUDAS ISCARIOT.

IN saintly guise he walked the land
As one of that devoted band
Whose self-denying lives afford
Repeated glimpses of our Lord.
He shared with them reproach and scorn,
From morn till eve, from eve till morn ;
But tempted sore by miser lust,
He sold his Lord, betrayed his trust.
Appalling space, the traitor fell,
From light to gloom, from heaven to hell !
Betrayer of the crucified,
A broken-hearted suicide !

But hatred, scorn and diatribe
Of earthly pen can ne'er describe
The anguish of that stricken heart,
Impaled by sorrow's piercing dart ;
No mortal hand can limn the trace
Of deep remorse that blanched his face ;
No human ear can catch the tones
Which marked the arch-betrayer's groans.
Oh ! think of his eternal doom,
Condemn'd for aye to deepest gloom ;
Whilst all men hate, despise, deride,
The dastard miser—Vaticide.

ST. HILDA'S BELLS.

ROM the pleasant vale of Whitby, by the German Ocean
   shore,
Floats the sweetness of a legend handed down from days of yore,
When that hardy North Sea rover, Oscar Olaf, son of Sweyn,
Swooping down on Whitby's convent, bore her bells beyond the
   main.
Far away to where the headlands on the Scandinavian shore,
With reverberating thunder—echo Baltic's sullen roar ;
      And sad the night-winds o'er the Yorkshire fells,
      Bemoan'd the absence of St. Hilda's bells.

But the storms of Scandinavia (Dane and Viking's sea girt home),
Smote the Baltic's angry breakers, lash'd them into seething
   foam,
Whose white-crested, heaving mountains drove the ruddy-
   bearded Dane,
(Him the Saxons feared and hated, Oscar Olaf, son of Sweyn)
Drove him back to cloister'd Whitby, and the German Ocean
   wave,
Rolls and breaks with ceaseless moaning o'er the North Sea
   Rover's grave.
      Aye rolls and breaks, as when it moaned the knells,
      Of Oscar Olaf, and St. Hilda's bells.

Oft the nuns and mother abbess of St. Hilda's lofty fane,
Sighed to hear the silver chiming of the convent bells again ;
Oft the herdsman on the moorland, and the maiden on the lea,
Mourned the missing iron songsters borne away beyond the sea ;
For it seemed as though the accents of the dear old bells no
   more
Would be heard in pleasant Whitby by the German Ocean
   shore.
      That evermore the North Sea's surging swells
      Would drown the music of St. Hilda's bells.

Aves, Credos, Paternosters, pleaded at St. Hilda's shrine
(Sacred altar where the franklin's and the villein's prayers
    entwine),
These, and presents rich and goodly, to that convent old and
    quaint,
Touched the heart of good St. Hilda, Saxon Whitby's patron
    saint ;
And 'tis writ in fisher folk-lore at her word old Ocean bore
On his crest the ravished songsters, stranding them on Whitby's
    shore ;
    And oft again o'er Whitby's woodland dells,
    Was heard the sweetness of St. Hilda's bells.

Years have fled far down the ages since those nigh-forgotten
    times ;
But each New Year's Eve the waters echo back the convent
    chimes,
And 'tis said—the youth who hears them, ere the coming year
    has fled—
(Flinging single life behind him) shall have pressed the nuptial
    bed ;
Sweet belief and quaint old legend, wafting long-forgotten lore
From the pleasant vale of Whitby, by the German Ocean shore,
    Where strolls the ancient fisherman who tells
    Of Oscar Olaf, and St. Hilda's bells.

TO A MAPLE LEAF.

ONLY a fragile maple leaf,
    Thy life has swiftly pass'd away,
Each lovely hue, in bright relief
Has early faded in decay ;
And yet the chill autumnal breath
Leaves thee most beautiful in Death.

WHARFEDALE.

S WEETLY chime the Sabbath bells,
  O'er dear Wharfedale's lovely dells,
Calling youth and maiden fair
To the village house of prayer,
As they pass with thoughtful mien
Down the dear old village green.
Ah! often in my vigils lone
I hear the bells' sweet monotone.

Picturesque, 'neath elm trees tall
Stands the quaint old manor-hall,
O'er whose walls and gables gray
Centuries have passed away,
Leaving many a tragic trace
Of an ancient courtly race.
Yes! often at the dawn of day
I see its walls and gables gray.

Nestling in a woodland lane,
Lies the ive-clad village fane,
Where, with awe, God's Holy Word
In the choral chaunt is heard,
As the gloaming softly falls
On its weatherbeaten walls ;
Still, from the chancel-choir's refrain
I often catch a wand'ring strain.

Ye bells, hall, church, so far, yet near,
To me ye are forever dear,
And shall be—till the morning light
Breaks o'er the watches of that night,
When I—fulfilling His behest—
Shall in " God's Acre " find my rest.

LYING EPITAPHS.

THE parting beams of crimson eventide
   Flung golden glory o'er the country side,
As, pensively, I pass'd each narrow bed,
Beneath whose shade repose the silent dead.

'Twas the sweet, melancholy sunset hour
When wayworn hearts, by a mysterious power,
Are lifted from the world with gentle hand,
And drawn more closely to the Better Land.

Each marble shaft upraised its lofty crest
Bathed in the wondrous splendour of the west :
And when the calm of even fell around,
It seemed as tho' the place was hallowed ground.

In truth, 'twas more than passing fair, I ween,
As length'ning shadows fell athwart the scene,
And, blending with the sunset's golden dress,
Veiled evening's thousand-tinted loveliness.

In fancy I could see the falling tear,
The mourning friends, the tomb, the sable bier,
And hear the words of simple faith and trust,
Consigning earth to earth, and dust to dust.

Whilst gazing on that monumental scene,
I thought how good these sleepers must have been,
How sorrowful their friends at the sad doom
Which marked these loved ones for the silent tomb.

For every epitaph belauded so
The quiet folks who slept in death below,
Whose saintly lives had only been surpassed
By legatees who'd buried them " at last."

" What peaceful lives, what loving friends! " I said
Unto a white-haired man. He shook his head ;
And then, I grieve to say, I rather think
I saw that patriarchal stranger wink.

" Oh, yes," he said, " what peaceful, honest lives !
What faithful husbands, oh, what virtuous wives !
What heavenly-minded, fatherly papas !
What tender-hearted, motherly mammas !

" Don't you believe it, sir," this old man said,
" Not quiet so good were these belauded dead,
Marked by their absence were the goodly traits
Ascribed to these sweet ' lights of other days.'

" The tombstones here are neither more, nor less
Than eulogies on byegone wickedness,
For did one pitch in vales of vice his tent,
The grander here that scoundrel's monument.

" Behold that carving on the tombstone there
(An angel in the attitude of prayer),
And note those precious lines, which all but say
Below, *perfection* waits the judgment day.

" Perfection ? No. A low-lived, swindling cheat,
A hideous mass of mercantile deceit,
Who honoured nature's debt when life decayed,
The only debt the rascal ever paid.

" Here lies another saint, so good ! so pure ! a true
And charming pupil of La Fontaine, who
When fear waxed strong, and strength of lust grew faint,
Called in the church, reformed, and died a saint.

" And yet, this man was one of those old blocks
Whose hearts are harder than tbe Plymouth Rocks,
Where pilgrim fathers fell upon their knees,
And, rising, fell upon the Aborigines.

" Again, read this : ' Sacred to one whose life
Was innocent of all unseemly strife,
For many years he wooed the pious three,
But most of all he loved sweet charity.'

" A frigid lover of them all was he ;
He must have wooed them very cautiously,
For e'er he e'en a thought to Hymen gave,
Death stayed the farce, and wed him to the grave.

" Oh, I could say much more than I have said
About these same departed, vaunted dead,
But falling dews, and evening's fading light,
Warn me that I must go, and, sir, good night."

Astounded by his sneers, he left me there,
Somewhat surprised that one whose reverend air
Would seem to mark the calm philanthropist,
Should prove a melancholy pessimist.

But oft his words have pass'd my mental view,
And oh ! if what he said be really true,
Then are those epitaphs which strangers see
But lettered emblems of Hypocrisy.

And each of our " God's acres "—if 'tis so—
Is nothing save a marble-cutter's show,
And each " Here lies " the good, the great, the wise,
But upright stones of downright chiselled lies.

AT CHRISTMAS-TIDE.

OANING, moaning o'er the prairie, wail the chill December
　skies,
Silently the drifting hardens where a storm-beat wand'rer lies ;
Swift the weird-like shadows glooming in the fading light of day,
O'er a lone heart sadly dreaming of the old home far away ;
And he sees those well known faces, chasten'd by the hand of
　Time,
As they sit around the ingle, listening to the clang and rhyme
　　Of sweet-toned bells, that, far and wide,
　　Ring in the gladsome Christmas-tide.

Borne above the north winds sobbing—o'er the clashing of the
　bells—
Float the tones of quaint old carols, touching chords of memory's
　cells ;
But the blessèd vision passes ; silent now the sweet refrain,
And the horrors of the Frost King rise before his ken again ;
One more effort, onward stagg'ring, till before his ice-lash'd eyes,
Beams the log-wood's cheery welcome, and his wild, despairing
　cries
　　Are heard by joyous hearts that glide
　　In the settler's dance at Christmas-tide.

Lanterns flashing, hounds a-baying, where a swooning form is
　found ;
Stalwart men and bright-eyed maidens, in the firelight gathering
　round,
Listen to the wand'rer's story how he left his camp at morn,
Missed the trail, the blizzard's raging, how he lay, with strength
　outworn,
Till the storm had spent its fury, and the numbness of his limbs
Warned him of insidious slumber, which for aye the senses dims.
　　How but for them he should have died,
　　'Neath a shroud of ice at Christmas-tide.

Moaning, moaning, wails the north wind, and the moonbeams break and pale,
O'er a nestling, peaceful homestead, in a pleasant English vale;
And around its glowing ingle kneel a gentle household band,
Who are praying for a wanderer in a far-off foreign land;
Pray the mother, sire, and sisters, pray they for an only son,
Asking Heaven to shield, in mercy, him, the wayward absent one.
  And by that prayer is Death denied
  In the Western wilds at Christmas-tide.

NEW YEAR'S EVE.

THE dying year, at the supreme command,
 Fades slowly in the dim, weird shadow land
(That mystic home of Time's departed dead,
Whither the shades of bygone years have fled)—
Fading with all its actions in its train,
And sad-voiced memories alone remain
To chide the weary, drooping hearts that sigh
For wasted moments in the hours pass'd by.
Vows lightly made—ah! bitter to redeem—
Plans, roseate once, swift-faded as a dream;
Weak, erring souls, swerving from Duty's line,
Dead incense offer now at Honour's shrine;
And the fair moon, by gath'ring clouds o'ercast,
Looks down in sorrow on the wasted past,
As silent vesper-stricken shadows fall
And veil the year now fading past recall.

The midnight hour has struck. The old church bell
Has toll'd the past year's sad, departing knell;
And sounding o'er the ether sweet and clear
The gladsome chimings hail a new-born year,

And sorrow-soilzied hearts their kindred greet
As from the kirk they pass adown the street ;
The future scann'd, the bitter past reviewed,
The broken vow, and covenant renewed.
All vanished now the darkling care-worn trace
Of haunting retrospection's gloomy face ;
The Old Year's sadness, faded now from view,
Is merged within the brightness of the New,
And Luna, radiant Majesty of Night,
Floods the New Year with cloudless streams of light,
That pierce each shadow'd path, as though to cheer
The way-worn pilgrim through the coming year.

A GRAVEYARD IDYLL.

NIGH a forest in the Northland,
   Lies a city of the dead,
Where the sighing breezes murmur
   'Midst the branches overhead.

Murmur'd softly as I rambled,
   'Neath their pleasant, soothing shade,
Thinking of those silent sleepers,
   Who in death's cold arms are laid.

For my friend had often told me,
   " When each blossom sweetly blooms,
'Tis a goodly thing to wander,
   Meditating by the tombs."

Oft, he said, he loved to linger,
   Marking death's destroying hand,
And such walks had always drawn him
   Nearer to a better land.

Thus, this pleasant morn I rambled
  Through that city of the dead,
Where the sighing breezes murmur
  'Mongst the branches overhead.

And I thought of yon fair country,
  On whose far-off golden shore
Happy pilgrim forms do wander,
  Free from travail evermore.

Musing thus, the sound of footsteps
  Brought my fancies to an end,
And behold! I saw before me
  Him, mine own familiar friend :

Yes! I saw that high-toned pilgrim,
  As I saw the witching head
Of a strapping, black-eyed nurse girl.
  In that city of the dead.

But his thoughts were not of Heaven
  Nor about the better land,
For her lips were glued to "his'n,"
  And his arm her waist enspanned.

"Hum! Ahem! I softly tittered
  And I smiled to see his haste—
And to see that look unconscious,
  As he dropped that nurse girl's waist.

Ah! they looked two sickly pilgrims,
  And methinks I see them still,
As they vanished from the precincts,
  As they scooted down the hill.

"IT MIGHT HAVE BEEN."

SHE.

" WHEN night o'er gentle nature weaves her pall,
   And darkling weird-like shadows lengthen fast,
With sadden'd heart I tearfully recall
   The long-departed, sweetly bitter past,
      And, pierced by memory's arrow keen,
      I murmur low ' It might have been.'

" On recollection's easel, one dear face
   With fancy's airy brush I love to paint;
Ah! oftentimes at even-song I trace
   The well-loved features of an earthly saint;
      And, gazing on that tender mien,
      I breathe the thought ' It might have been.'

" Too well I know that never, nevermore
   Shall I behold, on earth, that long lost form;
Mayhap—sweet thought—we'll meet on yond fair shore
   Whose haven shelter's free from every storm,
      And, viewing that Elysian scene,
      Shall realize what ' might have been.' "

HE.

" By Jove! 'tis just as well, perhaps, that fate
   Has thwarted thus my once fastidious taste,
I ' might have been ' to-day, the hen-pecked mate
   Of thirty-six or forty round the waist,
      And squalling brats—oh! hideous scene—
      Are 'mongst the things that ' might have been.' "

JESMOND DENE.

No fairer spot can well be found,
    For picnic, tryst or camping-ground,
Than this sweet grove, whose leafy shade
Is still secure from woodman's blade;
White fleecy clouds its tree-tops cap
Whilst rippling wavelets gently lap.
And oft the lover's form is seen
Within thy walls, O Jesmond Dene!

PUBLIC FUNERALS.

Slow tolled the sad-voiced bells that summer's day
    For one whose hour of life had passed away;
And the black hearse, and carriages on every side,
Told all around a wealthy man had died.

A self-made man—all praise for that—but one
Who worshipped nothing, save his father's son,
Whose newly-bought escutcheon should have been
A mushroom rampant on a field of green.

Amongst the crowd of mourners there, I saw
The merchant, banker, and the man of law;
His doctor, too, was there—a sour old Turk—
Who, tailor-like, was *taking home his work*.

How sad those precious mourners seemed to me,
At least quite sad the scamps appeared to be;
Each of them wore a yard of crape, or so
(An aggregate of many *yards* of woe).

Along the line of march the gathered mob
Quizzed the procession as it passed. No sob
Or word of sorrow for the dead man there,
Stirred the soft current of the summer air.

Grief? Pshaw! Their presence there appeared to me
As savouring less of grief than vulgar glee,
I could have thrust each atom of distress
In either eye, nor seen one whit the less.

The grave is reached.   Beneath the upturned sod
He lay, whose soul had gone to meet its God ;
And grandly, reverently, that day was read
The sweetly solemn service for the dead.

Amen ! And you'd have thought a boiler burst,
To see the way those mournful swells dispersed,
From *grave* to gay they quickly changed the tune,
And raced like madmen for the first saloon.

Oh ! How those broken-hearted mourners ran
And left behind the fat old alderman,
Whose gorgeous high-toned paunch (surpassed by none)
Seemed Mayor and *Corporation* all in one.

Alas ! thought I, such rank indecency
In this our nineteenth century !
Are these the men who, one short hour ago
Seemed fitting types of broken-hearted woe ?

But really 'pon my honour, it was quite
A ludicrous, though an improper sight,
For he who'd erstwhile worn the saddest brow
Indulged the most in *smiles*, et cetera, now.

And so, methinks, whate'er my rank in life,
When, at the last, I pass from mortal strife,
I trust my modest sable coloured pall
Will never head a public funeral.

For now I know that mockery of woe
Is nothing, save an undertaker's show,
And all the grief spectators feel or see,
But blatant, blasphemous hypocrisy.

DULCE DOMUM.

A LEGEND OF WINCHESTER COLLEGE.

Dulce Domum! Sweetly Homeward! Loud the old, familiar strain,
Rolls its wondrous tide of sweetness o'er the hills, adown the plain,
Bearing happy thoughts of school-work, soon—oh ! bliss—to be resigned
For the pleasant, dear home-coming—hall and studies left behind ;
And the gentle night-wind wafts it, over mountain, vale and lea,
Whispering softly to the white cliffs, and the white cliffs to the sea
Echo back the glorious anthem ; once again, and yet again,
O'er the woodland slopes of Hampshire, roll the gladly sweet refrain :
        Dulce Domum! Sweetly Homeward!

Dulce Domum! Sweetly Homeward! But each word with anguish thrills
One lone heart beneath the shadows of the grand old " Evening Hills,"
One, whose melancholy features likeness to his dead sire's bear,

Round whose young life beams the halo of a sainted mother's
  prayer,
And the scorching tear-drop glistens, rising nigh beyond control,
For the iron of his sorrow pierces to his boyish soul,
Whilst the memories of his childhood o'er fond recollection throng
As he listens, in his sadness, to his schoolmates' gladsome song :
  Dulce Domum ! Sweetly Homeward !

Dulce Domum ! Sweetly Homeward ! Homeless he, with none
  to bless ;
Not for him the hearth of welcome, nor sweet sister's warm
  caress ;
Chill his classmate's careless good-bye on his heart despairing
  falls,
Doom'd to linger, through vacation, in St. Mary's dreary halls ;
Dreaming of his happier childhood, and his gentle mother's love,
Wondering, if she now beholds him, from her home in realms
  above.
But forever, and forever, through those weary nights of pain,
In his orphan ears are ringing bitter echoes of the strain :
  Dulce Domum ! Sweetly Homeward !

Dulce Domum ! Sweetly Homeward ! Soon the "long vaca-
  tion's" o'er,
One by one the lads come trooping back to college life once more,
But a face they've known is absent, and they hear, with bated
  breath,
How their sad-eyed little comrade sleeps th'unbroken sleep of
  Death.
Yes ; an angel voice had whispered at the hour of midnight,
  "Come,"
And the dear Lord, in His mercy, took the little orphan Home.
Bright and glad the angels' welcome, who had waited for him
  long,
But the brightest, the most joyous, was the *youngest* angel's song.
  Dulce Domum ! Sweetly Homeward !

TUTOR NON ULTOR. (1879.)

A RABID cry is sounding far and wide
   In English halls, and cotters' ingleside,
" Avenge dark Isandula's day of shame ;
Avenge the blow they struck at Britain's fame."
And vulture-like the press old England flood
With lust of war and thirst for Zulu blood,
Because, forsooth, they've dared to make a stand,
And fight like men for sun-beat Zululand.

Had they been Greek or Montenegrin braves,
Or Switzers beating back the Archduke's slaves,
Our hearts would thrill with admiration deep,
And o'er each fallen hero's fate would weep ;
But these are only Zulu-Kaffir hordes,
Meet victims they for brutal troopers' swords,
And England slips the blood-stained dogs of war
On Afric's fair, pellucid, wave-beat shore.

Alas ! for England's trenchant arm of might,
Alas ! for England's vaunted love of right,
If thoughts like these her statesmen's minds pervade,
If crimes like these her soldiers' arms degrade,
Each hecatomb of Zulu's warlike race
Will be a monument to her disgrace ;
And she, who now is Freedom's foremost friend,
Shall soon to Freedom's foremost foe descend.

May calm and juster counsels soon prevail,
And shouts for peace resound o'er hill and dale,
Then all the nations, far and wide, shall know
How England scorns to crush a vanquish'd foe ;
And when the day of white-robed peace shall dawn
On those who dear and absent comrades mourn
(As they with open hands their foemen greet),
Let God-like mercy season justice sweet.

THE MAN IN THE PARK.

ARGUMENT.—Lo! Summer is here and the voice of the park preacher is heard in the land.

WHEN the whispering tones of a Sabbath-kiss'd breeze
Sigh, with musical cadence, midst summer-crown'd trees,
When the rays of blest sunshine and Nature's own voice
Bid the trance-risen landscape in beauty rejoice,
When the azure resounds with the notes of the lark,
O! 'tis then that we gaze on " The man in the park."

Ah! " The man in the park," sirs, blest creature is he,
From the frailties of mortal he's perfectly free,
He's an alien, true, in the realm of success,
And a failure in life, tho' he sneers none the less
At all wealth—yet a sail in prosperity's bark
Would uncommonly tickle " The man in the park."

He can smash up agnostics with thundering knocks,
Or, with mis-applied logic, be heterodox ;
He can spout (tho' his nose be suspiciously red)
On a Temperance theme, till his hearers have fled ;
For to argue black's white, and to swear light is dark,
Is the undenied right of " The man in the park."

He blackguards the parsons, from first unto last,
With small hope for their future, less respect for their past ;
They are wastrels who drink the sweet wines to the lees,
And are less interested in souls than in fees,
Thus in bile, be he navvy, mechanic, or clerk,
He's " agin " Mother Church, is " The man in the park."

I thought him erratic, but esteem'd him sincere,
In his howlings on " Faith " and his strictures on beer ;
But one day, as I traversed a Don-watered vale,

I beheld " Black Maria " on her way to the gaol,
And the rogue who peep'd out from the bars of " The Ark "
Was that stumbler from grace yclept " The man in the park."

Yet I like him, the scamp, and his overworked tongue,
Though the force of his logic ne'er equals his lung ;
I admire so the man who can shame a bassoon,
Who can discount, in antics, a circus buffoon,
And I tender my thanks (Heav'n assoilzie the mark)
To the " idjut " who's known as " The man in the park."

POMP DE SCALLAWAG ; HIS TEMPTATION AND FALL.

IN Blackstock town there dwelt in state a darkey known to fame,
Who bore, with lardy-dardy grace, the fascinating name
Of Pompy Pushcart Blackamoor de Scallawag, Esquire,
An unsophisticated black, a most atrocious liar,
A lowly born philanthropist, who often came to grief,
" Bekase de white trash swar I hab de mohals ob a tief."

Yet Pompey was not always thus ; in bye-gone happy days,
He walked, with free and easy grace, by virtue's pleasant ways,
But—Eden like—the snake appeared—oh! heritage of shame—
A Church of England temperance man P. Scallawag became ;
(This wicked act was more than bad, 'twas sacrilegious too,
For him whom Nature made a black, these Church folks made a
    " Blue ").

As Prohibition's protegé, with brimstone, fire and sword
He bore the star-gemm'd Temperance flag before his colour'd
    horde ;
It was, said those who ought to know, a grand, a glorious sight
To see that tatter'd flag upheld by this sweet darkey " light " ;
And edifying, too, to hear him swar and howl and brag,
" De standard bearer ob dis host am P. De Scallawag."

But platform cheers and spouting clubs—by wicked tongues 'tis said—
Shook Pompey from his centrepoise, and turned his woolly head:
Tea-fights and muffin-struggles, too, could not be said to tend
Toward those paths of rectitude where truth and honour blend.
And so to steal and lie and cheat became the sole desire
Of Pompey Pushcart Blackamoor De Scallawag, Esquire.

His stomach yearned for fairer fields, and greener pastures new,
Which artless whim was granted in an (unsought) interview
With Blackstock's leading magistrate, who thought a change of scene,
Would *rusticate* this *polished black* by turning him to Green,
The seigneur of a " Moated Grange," whose tesselated halls
Held Scallawag three dreary months within its hallowed walls.

But time rolled on to liberty, which little change 'twould seem
Affected not this African's calm, philosophic dream,
.Of wooing Fortune's fickle smiles, by living on his wits,
And " articles of vertu," which consist in scraps and bits,
Whose costly repertoires compose a complicated mass
Of greens, old iron, rags and bones, and spifflicated glass.

He prowled *a round*, "upon *de square*," till wicked thoughts, alas!
Stole round this guileless son of Ham, who wrought in scraps and glass;
Ah ! eagerly his pouting lips, and wicked rolling eyes
Would twitch and gleam with all the force of honest enterprise.
Which little enterprise was this—"to leab de glass and rags,
And 'vest De Pushcart's capertal in cotton sacks and bags."

Alas ! " De Pushcart's capertal " did not amount to much
(The root of evil's mighty shy of Pomp's financing clutch),
Five little bills was all he had, an " mortgaged eb'ry cent,"
Three dollars "chalked" fur whiskey "straights," de balance due fur rent ;

But what cared he about " de rent," de rent must wait awhiles,
And as fur Grab, de landlord's frowns, Pomp took those out
    in " smiles."

As old John Bunyan quaintly says, " it fell upon a day,"
When hens delight to bark and bite, and " yaller " dogs to lay,
That Pompey Pushcart Blackamoor De Scallawag, Esquire,
That unsophisticated Nig—that most atrocious liar—
Cast wistful eyes upon some bags a few short moons ago,
When passing by the canvass works of Sackman, Jute & Co.

Pomp's guardian angel whispered low that pleasant morn in May;
" De fohman at de factory is,"—so all de Gentiles say,
" A moh'l an' a nice young man, a Plymuff brudder, too,
So min' yer P's and Q's, ole boy, is my device to yoh,
An' don't ye swar, nor obfuscate, nor gib yerself away,—
Yah, yah, but when ye git dem bags, yo'll not be fur astray."

Per Jove! Before the morn had fled, Pomp, with his little cart,
Was " circumtittivating " round dat Plymuff brudder's heart,
By telling him—in confidence—" ob all de legion host
Ob secks," he did " prefer and lub de Plymuff brudders most ;
Dey was gallopshus gen'l-men, de fohmost in de land,"
And Pomp " was proud to offer dem a culled brudder's hand."

Alas! no mortal tongue can tell how Pompey " nailed " the lot,
And by a *verbal* I. O. U. " *discharged* ' his little " *shot* ",
But, sad to say, that's all he paid, for never, never more,
Was seen that guileless troubadour, from Afric's verdant shore :
And soft " dat Plymuff brudder " sighs, " The martyr's stake
    and fire
Is nought to what *I'd* like to give P. Scallawag, Esquire."

AT THE VICARAGE GATE.

Iɴ a storm-shelter'd valley, the North Sea's refraining,
 Croons a lullaby soft to the bob-o-link's call,
And the will-o'-the-wisp of the corn-craik's complaining
 Is hush'd, for the shadows of eventide fall.
Oh ! how peaceful the scene, when all Nature is sleeping
 (Save the Monarch of Night, and his horn-crested mate),
And Memory alone, her fond vigil is keeping
 Beneath the old elm at the vicarage gate.

There the ivy-clad walls, and each time-beaten gable
 Shelter'd lives where affection and peace were entwined,
And Virtue was loved, nor was duty a fable,
 Where the Graces of Home are for ever enshrined ;
There the woes of the suff'rer found kindly redressing,
 And the latch was ajar, even early and late,
Aye, and often was heard the poor wanderer's blessing
 Beneath the old elm at the vicarage gate.

Ah ! so exquisite too, on the lawn heavy-laden
 With the sighs of the hawthorn and sweet mignonette,
When the shy-whisper'd " Yes " from the lips of the maiden
 Sealed a love that was pure and untinged with regret ;
And the clasp of the hand and the true lover's token
 Whilst the cloud-stricken moon would her splendour abate
As she veil'd from outsiders the vows all unspoken,
 Beneath the old elm at the vicarage gate.

In that far away valley fond memory lingers,
 And dwells on the forms that are gone evermore,
But oft, in the gloaming, their shadowy fingers
 Are beckoning on to Eternity's shore ;
And Hope, from the past, an effulgency borrows,
 To lighten the path of the pilgrims who wait
For the meeting with those who once mingled their sorrows
 Beneath the old elm at the vicarage gate.

NOTHING LIKE LEATHER.

HE pompous old parson walked down the High street
  To order new boots for his clerical feet ;
Whilst leaving his measure the bootmaker's heir
Passed by, with his feet—as per usual—bare.
" Aha ! " quoth the hope of the church in disdain,
" The shoemaker's son, the old saw's true again ! "
" Good sir," said the cobbler—uncommonly riled—
" Don't quote that old saw of the shoemaker's child,
For if shoemaker's children are always worst shod,
Then the brats of the parson know least about God ! "

THE HAPPY FAMILY.

'TWAS Summertide, and, slowly sinking low
  Behind the eternal hills, in crimson glow,
The setting sun was seeking golden rest,
Away beyond in regions of the West,
And as the day in evening dews declined—
Ere Father Sol his azure throne resigned—
The placid heart of Cabbagetown was stirred,
On every passing breeze a cry was heard
That thrilled with deep and soul entrancing joy
The scapegrace bosom of each College boy,
" Great Pandrum comes."

            Next day the anxious town,
From " Bummer Jones " to good old Deacon Brown,
Assembled in the glorious morning light,
To catch one brief, ecstatic (gratis) sight
Of prancing steeds and pious circus men,

Flanking each caravan and wild beast den,
In all the glittering pomp and panoply
Of Pandrum's circus and menagerie.

Now, later on, that pleasant summer night,
Old Deacon Brown, a godly Baptist light,
Strolled out, *immersed* in deep, distracting thought,
Debating if a Baptist deacon ought
To visit anything so very low
As the great Pandrum's mammoth circus show ;
But curiosity—that pert young jade,
Whose wiles o'ercome, with ease, both man and maid—
Impell'd the musing deacon's erring feet
Towards a quiet, half-a-dollar seat,
Where he—thus mused this man of holy mien—
Unseen could view the fascinating scene.
Alas ! the free display of female limbs
Distressed the little man of psalms and hymns,
And thrilled his rather consequential frame
With quickened pulse and truly virtuous shame.
He peeped—oh ! fie !—and blushed ; then peeped again
(Remember deacons are but mortal men,
E'en parsons sometimes leave the narrow way,
And in the pleasant, broader pastures stray).

He watched the little spotted clown at play,
The " Arab coursers " rear and prance and neigh ;
He saw the " Amazonian Rider " stoop,
Ere swiftly bounding through the tissued hoop ;
And ague smote his horror-stricken knees
When he beheld old Pandrum's great trapeze
Suspended o'er the vulgar, gaping crowd,
That stared, and quizzed, and fairly yelled aloud
With frenzied glee as red-haired Senor Pat
O'Rourke, the Andalusian Acrobat—

A famous Cork hidalgo ! an' you please—
Who cleft the air with graceful ease,
And—Jove-like—sat (as witness Homer's theme)
Enthroned above the noisy " gods," supreme,
The hero of the bawling crowd below,
Which, breathlessly, beheld the " Spaniard " throw
His lissom, sinew'd frame (without a fault)
In a blood-curdling double somersault,
And smile his thanks amid the frantic roars
And pealing thunders of well earn'd applause.

But neither Pat, nor Amazon nor clown
Could cloy the appetite of Deacon Brown,
Who—spite of all the laws of Baptistry—
Now entered Pandrum's great menagerie,
In which—securely caged—a motley crew
Of Natural History met his startled view ;
Alarm'd, he heard the wild, enthunder'd roars
Of kingly exiles from old Afric's shores,
And trembled in his boots beneath the cage
That stayed the savage grizzly's hateful rage ;
He thrilled before the mighty velvet paws
Whose sheaths embraced the Bengal's blood-stained claws.
He saw the somewhat lofty, sad giraffe,
He heard the hideous chacma's barking laugh,
And, thankfully, he felt that iron doors
Shut in the Cayman's keen, incisive jaws,
Which hungered for the chattering, ceaseless tide
Of bright-eyed youngster forms that mount and ride
And whack—with many a thoughtless dig and thump—
The patient Bactrian's duplicated hump.

He poked the agile, bounding kangaroo,
And teased the carmine-breasted cockatoo,

But spared the fat old hippopotamus
And mail-clad, single-horned rhinoceros
(Which proves our deacon held, without pretence,
A precious rarity called " common-sense ").
But that which fill'd his heart with most delight,
On this self-same, eventful summer's night,
Was Pandrum's famous " Happy Family "—
The boasted pride of the menagerie—
Where howling " yaller " dogs, and squeaking rats,
And caterwauling Charles James Thomas cats,
And timid little mice, and great baboons,
And artful, dodging, ring-tailed, cute racoons,
With savage wolves and mild-eyed, gentle sheep,
Lay down together, drink and eat and sleep
In edifying peace and harmony,
A really model " Happy Family,"
The even tenor of whose peaceful life
Is innocent of all unseemly strife.

Amazed and fairly speechless with delight
The good old deacon view'd the wondrous sight
With upturned looks, with every finger clasped,
And thus bereft of speech he faintly gasped,
" I never, hardly ev—"   But, pardon, friends ; no more
Quotations, if you please, from Pinafore.
Suffice it, then, if I but simply say
The good old Baptist deacon went his way
Abstractedly, as in a pleasant dream,
Regardless of the home-bound human stream
That thundered forth in vast tumultuous tide
Away before, behind and at his side,
And onward rushing, swept by devious ways
In one loud sounding wave of earnest praise
(Regarding Pandrum's " Happy Family,"

His circus and the great menagerie)
That beached Brown like a log upon the shore
Of his own treasured home and dry goods store.

O, pleasant, witching night of leafy June,
How softly beamed the sweet young virgin moon
O'er waving fields of swiftly ripening corn
That sighed for all the warmth of coming morn.
Hushed lay the weary songster on his nest,
All mankind (query) bathed in sensuous rest,
Excepting one good soul—old Deacon Brown,
The leading hard-shell Baptist in the town,
Who, sleepless, wrapp'd in *close communion* deep,
Ne'er even dreamed of wooing fickle sleep.
Sad thoughts of Christian theoretic sticks
(Who argue bricks are stones and stones are bricks)
Came creeping o'er his poor distracted brain,
And filled his honest heart with tender pain.
To think that wretched, internecine strife
Existed so in modern Christian life ?
And sadly mused how it could ever be
That Christian men and brethren don't agree
To live in mutual peace and harmony—
One friendly, Christian Happy Family !

Anon the gloomy shades of black-robed Night
Are slowly put to ignominious flight
By tiny streaklets of the silver'd dawn
(Sweet heralds of the gently rising Morn),
Whose pleasant, cooing zephyrs softly steep
The Deacon's weary form in precious sleep.
Yes, sleep, for he—ere Orient shed his beams—
Had wandered in the golden land of dreams.

He dreamed, deluded man, with much delight,
That he and ev'ry leading, " shining light "
Of all the different Christian sects had met ;
That each had promised each that he'd forget
The bitter past, and all their tenets flood
In loving universal Brotherhood,
Whose leading thought and principle should be —
.   .   .   .
Here, Discord smote the youthful " Family,"
For not a single brother would condone
One clause or principle except his own ;
And precious soon, the Deacon saw, alas !
The Christian household one chaotic mass.

He saw th' Episcopalian, upright, stand
With ramrod back, and scornful pointed hand
At stern-souled independent constancy
To narrow Congregational bigotry,
And, swiftly borne upon the sobbing wind,
He heard the rather true retort, " You'll find
The proud Episcopalian's foremost creed
Is stuck-up social pride, and miser greed."
A Presbyterian quizzed, as unrefined,
John Wesley's sweet, enthusiastic mind ;
A red-haired Quaker tried to trim the lights
By running down to earth baptismal rites ;
Which *friendly* speech stirred up our Deacon's pride,
That, quick as lightning's vivid flash, replied :
" Quaker, our doctrines we shall ne'er regret ;
Cold water, Friend, has never hurt us yet."
The recent Dogmas of the Vatican
Were voted down by all, save one old man,
Who really thought " Infallibility "
Would surely save the " busted " Family.

A Mormon could not, for his very life,
See how a man could live with but one wife ;
" What ! more than one ? " A Plymouth Brother said
(Whose ragged ears, and hair-denuded head
Shew'd plainly that his own domestic life
Was not quite free from sanctifying strife),
" Another wife ? Be silent. I'm no muff,
But one, I think, is more than quite enough."
The heir of Joseph Smith and Brigham Young,
Seeing each against him, wisely held his tongue,
Whilst all the others, leaving him, began
To jeer a young Salvation Army man,
Accompanied by a " Hallelujah lass,"
Whose noisy clamour horrified the mass ;
Which shuddered when the hallow'd name of prayer
Was desecrated by th' excited pair,
Whose dubious actions, somehow, raised the thought,
And justified the popular report,
That both were Ishmaels in the social scale
The woman from the streets, the man from gaol.

Now, wrangling in Dissension's hateful throes,
From words these Christian swells soon came to blows,
Until the recent Happy Family
Seemed, to our deacon, the epitome   ٠
Of battered " Christy stiffs," bedrabbled clothes,
Black, " bunged-up " eyes, and claret-coloured nose,
With frantic tearings down of treasured rites
By blood-stained pugilistic " shining lights,"
Whose only earthly object seemed to be
The decimation of the Family ;
And, truth to tell, our pious beacon light
Was no inert spectator of the fight ;
Right manfully he swell'd the bloo ly fray,

On this eventful, fratricidal day;
Until—oh! cruel fate—two heavy blows,
Intended for St. Peter's Roman nose
By sour-faced Calvin's trenchant arm of might,
And English Churchman, stalwart for the right,
Flew wide the saintly Peter, but, alas!
Hit Brown, who sank beneath this *coup de grace*.

The noonday sunlight streaming o'er the floor,
And anxious servant knocking at his door,
Recalled the warlike dreamer back to life,
From underneath the wrecks of party strife;
But sadly faded were the roseate hues
Of poor old Deacon Brown's Utopian views.
" No," sighed the good man, very mournfully,
" The different sects on earth will not agree;
In Heaven, ah! yes, in Heaven alone can be
One *bona fide* ' Happy Family.' "

THE PHILOSOPHY OF THE CLUBS.

WHEN one short month has ta'en the bloom off matrimonial life,
The dullest company in the world is Benedict's own wife.

To love your wife is happiness—the highest—but to be
Bereft of love for her, once lovèd, is supremest misery.

Replete with interest to all, our last bewitching flame
Whose chiefest charm is this, she's another's trusted dame.

The fascinating woman's never ours, never, for then
Her charms would pale away before the brides of other men.

The married butterfly's a card, who sipping, loves to roam,
Always at home save when, alas! the rascal *is* at home.

The honeymoon is passing sweet.   Oh, hollow! hollow! hollow!
'Tis only sweet compared unto the bitter days that follow.

The highest matrimonial bliss, our wisest men have said,
Dwelt in the peaceful mind of him, who pass'd from life unwed.

Two silent women walked the earth, with calm perfection's tread,
The one has never yet been seen—the other's long since dead.

Men love but little here below, mere trifles light as air,
And dote upon their club because there are no women there.

IN MEMORIAM.

DEAN GRASETT.

HE sleeps his last sleep, and bedimmed is the gladness,
    That beamed with the light of his spirit's sweet bloom ;
All silent his voice, whilst the fount of our sadness
    Bedews with its pathos the flowers on his tomb.
But not without hope, e'en though earth now retaineth
    His body of clay 'neath her storm-beaten sod ;
Enshrined in our hearts his dear memory remaineth,
    Whilst he has returned to Jehovah, his God.

Departed to rest ere the bright day's declining
    Had crimsoned the west with its bright, saffron'd blush,
With loved ones beholding his manhood resigning
    Its exquisite beauty in Death's pallid hush.
But the pale horse's rider of dread ne'er appalled him
    (The fathers in Israel are strangers to fear),
He knew 'twas the Master at eventide called him
    Away from the toils of his pilgrimage here.

He's gone from our midst, but a halo still lingers
   Encircling his name with Consistency's light,
His life and example, like bright angels' fingers,
   Are pointing to regions where day has no night.
O soldier of Christ, ne'er thy worth shall we know here,
   Esteeming each cross but a labour of love.
'Tis well. Though one less in the army below here,
   One more is enrolled in the legions above.

He sleeps his last sleep, and the tempest's wild story
   Shall wail forth its woe o'er the place of his rest,
Yet we know, oh! so well, that the dwellers in glory
   Behold him reclining on Jesus' dear breast.
Oh! may this sweet knowledge assuage our deep sorrow
   For he—whom we mourn—has but gone on before,
And safe, in the Kingdom, awaits the fair morrow
   That dawns on our meeting on Heaven's bright shore.

DR. TANNER'S FAST.

INANE, self-glorious lunatic! thy name
   Has swelled the mulish bray of bastard-fame,
As that of one who immolates himself
Beneath the Juggernaut of miser pelf;
How beautiful the pure æsthetic taste
That marks thy forty days of tissued waste!
Thy blasphemous and idiotic fast,
In lunacy, can only be surpassed
By fools and quacks, who linger round the bed
Of one, whose stomach's empty as his head.

June, 1879.

FROM GLOOM TO LIGHT.

[Some years after the Restoration, an aged cavalier—whose sons had died fighting for the lost cause, whose estates had been confiscated during the Protectorate, and whose claims for past services had been ignored by the worthless Court of the second Charles—entered Lincoln Cathedral to pray.]

EXILED from Hope, all gloomy seems my way,
    O'er my dark life Despair holds bitter sway,
  As, bending low beneath my cross of sadness,
I seek, with aching heart, the aisles of prayer ;
    For oh ! methinks the rays of joy and gladness
Can never pierce the gloom of my despair.

And, as I slowly pace the column'd aisle
That cleaves in twain this grey, historic pile,
  The vast cathedral, bathed in golden glory,
Reflects fair evening's carmine-tinted sky
    Athwart the chancel window's painted story
Of One who for our surety came to die.

As the soft trilling of a wayside stream
With gentle murmur soothes the wand'rer's dream,
  Fall the loved tones of Him, the meek and lowly,
Borne on the anthem's sweetness to mine ear,
    Telling how He, the Lord of Heaven, most holy,
Is, if I only trust Him, ever near.

How small my sorrows seem compared with those
Whose awful ending bore dark Calvary's woes.
    My earthly lands and home I lost. With sorrow
And a grudging heart I saw them pass away ;
    But He resigned a throne whose glorious morrow
Welcomes the heart that scorns its King to-day.

Slowly the waning streams of golden light
Merge in the shadows of descending night;
   As Hope, at Faith's low call, comes softly stealing
From the fair mansions of the truly blest,
   And, as I bend in supplication kneeling,
Soothes all my gloomy doubts and fears to rest.

What care I now, tho' outward shadows fall,
For now I know, ah! me, so well, that all
   Those dreadful mists of gloom and doubt which shaded
The landscape of my heart, so long o'ercast,
   Beneath the sunshine of His love have faded
In the receding outline of the past.

.   .   .   .

As the weird gloaming weaves the shroud of day,
His parting breath in silence passed away;
   And the great organ's grandly solemn pealing
And soften'd cadence swelled unnoticed where
   The moon's pale beams of silver fell, revealing
A suppliant in the attitude of prayer,
       Whose soul had fled this vale of woe
       To meet the loved of long ago.

AT THE TROCADERO.

SHE pass'd, in beauty, down the column'd way,
   Where pulsing music on the ether floats,
In am'rous melodies, that kiss the spray,
   And woo the plashing fountain's dreamy notes.

Her starry eyes were heaven's own azure blue,
   Her hair, like to the mediæval saint,
Whose amber'd glistening threads of golden hue
   The old Florentine master loved to paint,

And, as she pass'd, each held his breath, and vowed
  Her peerless. All save one, a mushroom clod,
That with vile, lecherous leer, exclaim'd aloud,
  To all assembled there, " Painted, by g—d ! "

She heard, and hearing, bent her stately head,
  A gentlewoman's accent in each tone,
As, turning to that soul of clay, she said—
  " Painted by God, and, sir, by Him alone."

Paris, 1887.

———

SONNET TO A MULE.

ILLUSTRIOUS pledge of lawless amorousness !
  Celestial kicker !—Pray assuage the ire
That threatens from those shifting orbs of fire
Sweet foretaste of a saintly heel's caress.
Yet, Muley, each who views thee must confess
Thou hast the peaceful virtues of thy sire ;
Those intellectual hoofs would ne'er desire
To spifflicate the spirit of the press.
In peace I titillate thine hide, and, lo !
I grasp thy tail, and—thud ! ouch ! all things melt,
And stars and meteoric showers glow
Above a blighted liverpad ! and oh !
Good Christians, go and feel what I have felt,
Cycloned by hybrid heels " below the belt."

HOW THE CHILDREN SAVED NAUMBURG.

CALM the harvest moon is beaming on fair Naumburg's vine-
    girt plain,
Where the Säale-Unstrut waters blend in tribute to the main.

But, within beleaugured Naumburg utter woe each heart enthralls,
For the dreaded Hussite captain circumvents her ancient walls.

Prokop, terror of Bohemia, with a heart distilled in hate
'Gainst those towns whose vengeful judgment urged his martyr'd
    leader's fate.

Had not Naumburg swelled that council which, for Mother
    Church's sake,
Lured John Huss from old Bohemia, ere it doomed him to the
    stake ?

And the people send their elders unto Prokop's camp, to plead
For the goodly town and vineyards, in their solemn hour of need.

" Dear to us these scenes of childhood (sad the pathos of their
    wail),
For the ashes of our fathers rest within this peaceful vale."

Fierce the ire of Andrew Prokop, and his fury-quicken'd breath
Hisses forth : " For Naumburg, Mercy wears the sable garb of
    Death.

" Meet it is, ye men of Naumburg, I should put to fire and sword
Her who, by her wicked counsels, slew th' anointed of the
    Lord."

Deep the voice of lamentation, loud the women's answering wail,
When the weeping fathers tell them that their prayers have no
    avail.

Visions dark of sack and rapine fill with cries the stricken
    air,
And the hellish lust of murder seems already rampant there.

Weep, O matrons! Shriek, ye maidens! Sob, frail infants at the
    breast!
Soon the swooping carrion's scream shall desecrate your bloody
    rest.

But amid the cries and tumult born of Naumburg's bitter woe,
Speaks old Caspar, the schoolmaster, white with seventy winters'
    snow.

"Youth may fade. The agèd *must* die. Death to me were little
    loss;
Gather all the little children; rally at the market cross.

"I will lead them unto Prokop through the guarded southern
    gate,
And their prayers shall, by His blessing, stay our vengeful foe-
    man's hate."

"What!" the mothers cry in anguish, "lead our lambs into the
    den
Of the wolfish Hussite, Prokop, fiercest of the sons of men!

"Yet, alas! they're doomed as surely an' they stay till Naum-
    burg's won;
Take them, lead them to the Hussites, and the good God's will
    be done."

Passing fair that frail procession, waving palms with childish
    mirth,
Scatt'ring flowers—God's sweetest kisses to His children on this
    earth.

Waving palms, and scattering flowers, on their mercy mission
  bent,
Past the outworks, past the soldiers, till they come to Prokop's
  tent.

"Listen to our prayer, dread chieftain! Stay, oh! stay the
  conquering hand ;
Spare the hearths and lives of Naumburg, spare our dear old
  Fatherland."

Sing they from—sweet children voices—hymnals of their Gothic
  fane,
Rich in mediæval sculpture, carved in a forgotten reign.

Wrath, amazement and compassion stir the depths of Prokop's
  heart,
But the frown of dark displeasure brightens where the tear-drops
  start.

Like unto his little Anna's, one sweet face sad mem'ry thrills,
Gentle Anna, peaceful sleeping 'neath the far Moravian hills.

Lifts he in his arms that frail one, he the Pope and Kaiser feared,
And his soldiers cheer the prattler as it grasps their leader's
  beard.

"Go your ways, sweet little children, ye have won your town's
  release ;
Prokop's forces enter Naumburg, but they pass her gates in
  peace."

And the mother's tear-dimm'd vision sees the entering Hussite
  band
Lead her children to the elders, greeting them with open hand.

  .   .   .   .

Thus the children saved old Naumburg from the red right hand
of War,
And the baffled vulture's screaming vexed her peaceful vale no
more.

Calm the harvest moon is beaming on fair Naumburg's vine-
girt plain,
Where the Säale-Unstrut waters blend in tribute to the main.

Säale-Unstrut, roll your waters! Sing your ever ceaseless rhyme!
Comrades of the passing ages in th' eternal march of Time!

HIS ARTIST-SOUL RETURNED.

THE solemn hour of pensive evensong
Flush'd o'er an artist who had tarried long
In vain attempt to limn a pastoral scene.
Alas! the power was fled that once had been,
And—youth is passionate—pale anger's serf
In fury flung himself upon the turf,
And sobbed in mingled ire and mental pain,
" Heav'n give me back my artist-soul again."

" Heav'n give me back my artist-soul again."
The woods and song-birds heard the sad refrain,
And so did Mangelwurzel's Durham steer
That charged the unsuspecting mourner's rear,
And fired him o'er the fence upon the head
Of the old darkey tramp, who softly said,
Beneath the boot that struck the listening black:
" Befoah de Lawd, dat artis' *sohl's* kim back."

SCAMPKOWSKI.

SCAMPKOWSKI was a Polish Jew, a friendless refugee;
   Although he called himself a Count, not much account
      was he,
Until our Church converted him, and, with a helping hand,
Snatched him from fierce Judean flames—an exhibition brand ;
Raised him from dark Mosaic depths, where Jewry toils and
   delves,
And held him up to public view, a Christian, like ourselves;
Yea ! how we petted that young Pole, from o'er the North
   Sea's foam
(A foreign heathen's nicer than the pagans born at home).

His voice was lifted up in praise ; in prayer he wrestled long ;
And, did a tea-fight fiercely rage, Scampkowski loomed up
   strong ;
Or, was a widow in distress, or sick an orphan brat,
Although he never gave, himself, he "handed round the hat."
" How good he is," we often said, on this point all agreed,
And when he heard himself announced by one consent decreed
As Hon'ry Treas'rer of the Widows' and the Orphans' Fund,
He blushed, and blushing looked as though his very soul was
   stunned.

Among his philanthropic deeds we church folks had to thank
Scampkowski's fertile genius for our " Penny Savings Bank ";
And, verily it seemed to us a pleasant, goodly sight,
When workingmen flocked to our bank on every Friday night,
Depositing their gains, instead of spending all in drink,
And, raking in their little all, we each one used to think
Scampkowski's face divine, as unctiously he said (how true);
He " tankt de Lor vat mait me von convairted Polees Shoo."

And when that pious refugee had left for parts unknown,
Although our church's debt remained, the communion plate
  was gone ;
The Widows' and the Orphans' Fund, which *once* was *now* was
  not,
The Savings Bank deposits, too, had shared an exile's lot ;
And our parson's bitter, heartfelt words no mortal tongue can
  say,
When he found the offertories gone for ever and a day.
As sidesman Jones, the *dentist*, said, " I never liked him, still
Scampkowski's left an *aching void* which no one else can *fill*.

THE DEATH OF BURNABY.

"CLOSE up in front, and steady, lads ! " brave Stewart cries,
    " They're here " :
And distant Cheops echoes back our soldiers' answering cheer ;
One moment's pause—a year it seems—and swift the Arab horde
Pours forth its mingled tide of hate and yells and spear and sword;
As demons fight, so fight the children of the desert plain,
Their naked breasts defy our steel again and yet again ;
But steady as the granite cliff that stems a raging sea,
Above the van of battle looms our " Bayard "—Burnaby.

Broken! The square is pierced ! But only for a moment,
  though,
And shoulder-strap to shoulder-strap our brave lads meet the foe ;
And on this day the Bedouin learns, in the Mahdi's shatter'd
  might,
With what a God-like majesty the island legions fight.
But, oh ! the cost, the bitter cost ! for ere the set of sun
The bravest heart of Alba's isle its earthly course has run ;
And Britain weeps sad, bitter tears whilst flushed with victory,
For on Metemneh's blood-red sand lies noble Burnaby.

Avenged ? Behold what hecatombs around the dead man lay
(The royal paw is heaviest when the lion's brought to bay) ;
And as the shades of even fall upon this day of strife
That heap of slain exceedeth far the foes he slew in life.
And when a sneering alien tongue shall speak of him with scorn,
Or hint at our decaying might, the child as yet unborn
Shall beard the dastard to his teeth, and tell exultingly
How like the Israelite in death was " Samson " Burnaby.

Intriguing Russia's prestige waned in far-off Persia's State
When England's lonely horseman stood at Khiva's guarded gate,
Ay ! Bruin of the northern steppes, roll forth thy fœtid breath :
Exult, since now that lion heart is stilled for aye in death ;
And scream thine hate, proud bird of France, beyond thy
    northern shore,
Perfidious Albion drapes her halls for one who is no more.
Farewell, the last and brightest star of England's chivalry,
'Neath Orient skies thou sleepest well, O gallant Burnaby !

THE VALE OF LUNE.

Far beyond the blue Laurentians, past yon bleak, unhappy
    shore
(Altar shrine of Desolation—savage wilds of Labrador),
'Yond Atlanta's night of waters, borne on pensive Fancy's
    breeze,
Speed my thoughts to where old ocean laves the white isle of
    the seas ;
And I see old England's towers, bulwarks 'gainst the century's
    blast,
That amidst her halls of labor, blend the present with the past ;
But to exiled heart the dearest, sweet as summer's wayside rune,
Is the murmur of the waters in the little Vale of Lune.

Sheltered by the Pennine shadows, lags the drowsy waterwheel,
By the weir a big kingfisher watches for his morning meal ;
E'en the broad stream's sinuous current has a lingering tranquil
glide,
As tho' loth to leave those summits whence had burst its silver
tide ;
And two figures shade the archway, where it spans the old
mill-race,
Which are like to Dick, the keeper, and the miller's daughter,
Grace.
Oft, I trow, do twilight shadows and the chaste young harvest
moon,
Listen to the old, old story, in the happy Vale of Lune.

There the hoary ive-clad tower and the churchyard's honoured
dust
(Sleeping till the night of ages shall redeem its sacred trust),
And, hard by, where "rock" and "fantail" haunt its many-
gabled roof.
Stands the pleasant little ale-house, ancient, but still weather-
proof.
There the village politician, in his own peculiar way,
Settles home and foreign troubles in short order every day ;
Yes, the problems of a nation can be worked out wond'rous soon,
By the statesmen of that ale-house in the sunny Vale of Lune.

As of yore a group of matrons linger at the moss-crowned well,
What a tale of homely gossip do those honest gestures tell !
And how quaint their simple curtseys as the rector checks his
pace,
Asking for some ailing goodman (missed from his accustomed
place
When the peaceful Sabbath stillness—happy truce to worldly
care—
And the belfry's tuneful voice had called the hamlet unto prayer)!
Ay, the wearers of the kirtle and the lowly wooden shoon,
Have a kind word for the parson in the pleasant Vale of Lune.

Ye may traverse Alpine ranges, dream your dreams 'neath
    southern skies,
On fair Rhineland's halls and legends feast your travel-sated
    eyes,
Laud Niagara's foam-clad torrent, Chaudière's tumultuous wave,
Thundering an eternal requiem for the bye-gone Indian brave;
I have seen them, I have known them, but my heart and halting
    breath
Thrill and sigh for one more humble, and I ask of thee, O, Death!
When thy shadows close around me, grant me but one parting
    boon,
'Tis to sleep thy dreamless slumber in the peaceful Vale of Lune.

THE LORD MAYOR OF YORK AND HIS BROTHER NED.

ONE day—no matter what the date—
    The unrelenting hand of Fate
An uncommercial traveller took,
Sans sample case and order-book,
To York, whose time-worn Minster-Fane
Was built in—I forget whose reign;
And 'neath whose walls the vaults encrust
The warlike Thurstan's martial dust,
And legions, too, of sainted dead,
Of whom, by slanderous tongues, 'tis said
That they, tho' Mother Church's tools,
Were really more of knaves than fools,
Who, after lives of war and lust,
Through gifts were numbered with the just;
The Church transcribed their epilogues,
And canonized the mouldering rogues.

But love for antiquated lore,
And scandal's charms must not ignore
Our gentle uncommercial friend,
Who, having reached his journey's end,
Cigar in mouth, with outstretched feet,
Is gazing down the busy street ;
The smoke between his pearly teeth
In azure-tinted circles wreath.
In truth he seems, reclining there,
The living type of anti-care.
Anon, he starts ; then steps to greet
A peddler riding down the street,
With donkey-cart and crockeryware,
All bound for Pickering's yearly fair,
(Whose cash returns would greatly shame
Some fairs of more ambitious name.)

" Ha ! what's the row ? " the peddler cries,
" One moment, please," our friend replies,
" Before you take that beast away,
A word with him I wish to say."
The clown returns with calm repose
(His digits stealing to his nose),
" A crown I'll take to crown your joke,
And quick ere I the chance revoke."
The coin is paid, the cad meanwhiles
Retires, his face enwreathed in smiles.
Whilst our old friend (with pulled back cuffs,
And weed, inhaled with vigorour puffs)
Approached the peddler's long-eared steed,
The ashes flicking off the weed,
And then—excuse a manly tear—
The burning mass rammed down its ear.

A snort, a yell, a runaway,
With Hades' King and more to pay ;
That donkey's sentiment seemed clear
For—*entre nous*—an ass's ear,
The weakest part is said to be
Of asinine anatomy ;
And in pursuit there swiftly ran
A mad, blaspheming, crockery man,
Whilst pot and pan and looking-glass
Were smashed by that erratic ass,
Who showed astounding powers of speed,
Though not an ass of " Ukraine " breed ;
And yet it is but fair to state
He showed a clear 1.90 gait ;
Indeed, unbroken stands to-day,
The record of that runaway.

But all things earthly have an end,
(That they should not " the saints forefend ")—
And no exception to the rule
Was this half-brother of a mule,
Who, scorning pots and frying-pans,
Soon reached the ancient bridge which spans
The hollow bed where deep and slow
The Ouse's classic waters flow ;
But frightened by a passing team,
He leaped the bridge and charged the stream,
Whose turbid waters, soon, alas !
For aye closed o'er that luckless ass.
Oh ! loud his owner stormed, and swore
He'd " bring the case before the law,"
Ne'er dreaming that a red-hot weed
Had caused the sad, disastrous deed.

Next day before the civic chair,
(In other words—my lord, the Mayor)—
Our uncommercial friend was sued
" In that he did deceive, delude
An unsuspecting working-man
That dealt in pot and frying-pan,
And who, with many a mournful wail
And sigh, relates the dismal tale,
Whereby the goods for Pickering fair
Are numbered with the things that were.
Up jumped our friend, and then and there
Explained the case before the Mayor,
And proved there was a bargain made,
And that the promised cash was paid.
" Tut, tut, my man," quoth York's Lord Mayor,
" Dismissed, absurd, the whole affair."

The case dismissed, on leaving court
My Lord, the Mayor, our traveller sought,
" I really, sir, should like to know
What made you treat that donkey so.
Now what on earth had you to say
That he should act in such a way ? "
" Indeed, my lord, I must confess
'Twill cause your lordship much distress,
Yet, if you wish it, I'll relate
The cause of his untimely fate.
I went to him and simply said :
' What ! carrying pots—disgraceful ! Ned,
A general monger's drudge—and you
The Mayor of York's twin brother, too !
Well, blow me tight, but here's a go,
How could you shame his lordship so ? '

" Now, when I spoke he shook his head,
And, sighing mournfully, he said :
' Alas ! I long have felt that we
Were born in close affinity ;
Here goes ! no longer will I wear
This ignominous earthenwear,
No ! in the river's gentle stream
I'll close for good Life's transient dream.'
With that, my lord, he took to flight,
And passed away from mortal sight.
'Tis only just that you should know
'Twas shame that laid your *brother* low,
For, seeing you the child of Fame,
And he an ass of humble name,
The rest and silence of the dead
Were sought by that poor quadruped."

Alas ! the incandescent joke
Which killed that donkey—yclept a " Moke "—
Caused York a vacant civic chair,
For he who'd filled the post of Mayor
Was *cowed* so much that to this day
He promenades the " Milky Way "
(Whose pale, ethereal bar of light
Adorns the star-gemmed hours of night);
Where, far removed from mortal view,
He emulates the Wandering Jew,
But everlastingly avoids
The neighbourhood of *A*steroids.

GETHSEMANE.

A GARDEN in an eastern vale,
  Where silver'd moonbeams break and pale
In crystal waves of light, that gleam
On Kedron's brook, o'er Siloam's stream,
Where flow'rets bloom perennially—
The garden of Gethsemane.

In silence, as the fading light
Sinks slowly in the shades of night,
A form appears upon the scene,
Whose suffering heart and heavy mien
Proclaim, with silent majesty,
The Lord of fair Gethsemane.

Behold! 'Tis He; the Lord of Life
Wrestling in agonizing strife;
In strife whose victory breaks the spell
That binds mankind to death and hell
In strife whose cup and agony
Immortalize Gethsemane.

"Father! If 'tis Thy will, this day
Take, take my cup of woe away;
Yet, Father—prays Thine only Son—
Not My will, Lord, but Thine be done."
And soft the night wind, pityingly,
Wails sadly o'er Gethsemane.

Ye shaded groves of leafy palm
Enshrined in twilight's holy calm!
What mortal heart can e'er regret
His agony and bloody sweat
When angels laud, adoringly,
Yon hour in sad Gethsemane.

And in the dark and lonely hour,
When clouds of bitter sorrow lour,
The mem'ry of that emptied cup
Shall bear the burden'd spirit up
To Him Who gained the victory
Within thy walls, Gethsemane !

CHELLOW DENE.

WIND of the North !—blanching the fields of green—
  What of the shadowed hour of Chellow Dene ?
A lover has whispered a last good night,
  By the verge of Chellow's wave ;
But the green orb is nigh, and the sad winds sigh
  O'er a lover's nameless grave ;
And a murderer rides at a furious pace,
  For well, oh ! full well, knows he
That the son of his sire, in a bloody attire,
  Is sleeping all peacefully.

Wind of the South !—sighing at lang'rous e'en—
What of a heart that once knew Chellow Dene ?
  A Red-cross nurse, where the vine-clad walls
    Slope down to a Southern sea ;
  One nurtured in ease, who has drained to the lees
    Of the chalice of misery.
  Oh ! her pure, sweet face in the sunset glow
    Is wreathed in a golden gleam,
  And her deft hand's caress sooths the weariness
    Of a dying soldier's dream.

Wind of the West !—pulsing each prairie scene—
What of the serpent's trail from Chellow Dene ?
  Bound hand and foot by the Vigilants
    In the land of the setting sun,
  There is one swings on high, and his lustreless eye
    Is the thread of a life that is spun.
  To the horse thief, the gambler, and fratricide,
    Short shrift and a hempen rope ;
  For Death ever steals upon judgment's heels
    On the far Pacific slope.

GUILIA'S PRAYER.

MADONNA ! gentle mother, virgin undefiled,
  At Heaven's high throne plead for my little child,
Breathe o'er his languid frame thy healing balm,
And shield ! oh, shield ! my little one from harm.

The night of Death hath pass'd, its shadows flee
And joy fills all my heart, for now I see
The Lord of Life has gazed on thee, and smiled,
And kiss'd thy lips, my own, my darling child.

THE MISSIONARY SHIP.

DIVERS moons have waxed and waned, since yon night my
    erring feet
Wander'd nigh a place of worship adown a quiet street,
And the good folks pass'd those portals—redolent of prayer and
    praise—
Pass'd in scores—nay, by the hundred—before my wondering
    gaze :

Curiosity's my weakness (a weakness which be pleased to note,
Lures us as it fondly lureth the festive petticoat),
And I entered where the archway aloft this legend bore,
" Welcome! Missionary Ship! Bound for far-off Labrador."

In a space, hard by the pulpit, there rode a model ship,
Mann'd and rigg'd in all the latest for her missionary trip ;
Flanking either side were coffers—here the vulgar and refined
Left the tissued root of evil, or materials in kind.
Honoured he who gave a fiver—most honoured—saving when
Some rich sinner " went him better " with a greasy looking X ;
Till, as I view'd that oily pastor, methought that there were
    more
Poorer folk amongst my neighbours than the swells of Labrador.

Labrador being in the tropics, as every schoolboy knows,
May account for the abundant supply of summer clothes ;
Sensible donations were they, so picturesquely light,
Breathing thoughts of airy noonings, and the balmy hours of
    night.
And one dear, old giddy spinster, who succours orphan cats,
Touched my heart to see her bundle containing garden hats ;
How the sultry youth and . maiden, lingering by their native
    shore,
Hold her name in deepest reverence in sun-beat Labrador.

Now the only thing which troubled that noble-minded band
Was the somewhat handsome balance of cash they held in hand ;
Parents in Israel they, to spend, " in kind," 'twere surely best,
For who *can* judge of Eastern wants like the good folk of the
    West ?
Yes ! this seemed the proper caper, and they bought a lot of those
Drab puggarees, mosquito-nets, fans, and other Arctic clothes ;
And Heav'n will bless that *pastry-cook*, who 'umbly 'eld the floor,
And moved a ton of *ice-creams* be sent to Labrador.

LENTEN-TIDE.

ᵀELL me, O spirit of my heart, why lays
  The pall of silence on the bier of mirth ?
Why mem'ry's sigh for pleasant byegone days
That unto men gave laughter happy birth ?
Why gloom within thy halls, Terpsichore,
And erstwhile flesh of beasts to us denied ?
Oh wherefore thus ? Kind spirit ! whisper me—
And low the spirit pityingly, replied,
  " Because, my son, 'tis Lenten-tide."

BELAY ! BELAY THERE !

ᵂITH a clang and a bang, from the steeple is calling
  The voice of the bell—rising higher and higher—
But its bang and its clang is as naught to the squalling
Of the belle o' the church who sits with the choir.

EXACTLY SO.

ᴼNE nuisance Father Adam missed
  In the brave old days of yore,
He wasn't asked by Mother Eve,
  " Have you ever loved before ? "

Jack seldom wears his dressing-gown,
  You ask me " Why ? "—it maybe !—
Because the pattern is so loud
  It always wakes the baby.

Intestate died that miser Flint,
  Who lived like a hermit—alone,
Intestate, yes, but none deny
  He'd always a *will* of his own.

OUR LITTLE DICK.

I AREN'T no skollard, sir, miself, but them as knose do say
Our eddycashun sistem is the finest knone to-day;
An' me, an' my old wummun thort as 'ow lukky 'twos for Dick
To larn to rite like coppur-plate, an' swaller rethmetick.

Ah! wot a clever chap 'ee wos, that little lad o' ours;
Wy! larnin' seemed as nort to 'im, 'ee'd sich huncommon powers,
Lawks! 'ow 'ee rattl'd orf 'is sums—main prowd was I and glad
To see 'im nock the spots orf me, 'is pore old Hinglish dad.

'Is teechurs they was prowd of 'im—they swared 'ee'd some day be
A horniment to hall the frends of sich'n a projidy!
An' so they cram'd 'is nights wi' tasks, an' more when them wos
dun;
Ah! surely it wos kind o' them to 'elp a pore man's son.

An' bi-an'-bi they rush'd 'im thro' them 'igh-flone classick wurks
Wot tells of Joolyus Seezer's fites, as welted 'eathin Turks,
Corneelyus Nippers—Verjil—an' 'is nibs, old Tashytuss,
An' Neerow, an' a 'ost besides, wot hacted skandylus.

Sometimes my missus thort as Dick wur lookin' summat pale,
An' sed 'is 'elthy happytite 'ad some'ow seemed to fale;
It bothered 'er to see our lad gro' thinner bit by bit,
An' feel 'is 'ed as 'ot as fire, an' akin fit ter splitt.

But them kind teechurs laft at 'er an' sed as 'ow that they
Must 'ave 'im studdy on until hexaminashun day;
An' 'sed as 'elthy, wel-grone lads was sekond in *thare* heyes,
To pail-faced stoodyus chaps like Dick, wot took the 'ighest prise.

Summow 'ee kep' on loosin' strength, an' turn'd so downrite hill
We 'ad to keep 'im hin 'is bed—ware o' corse 'ee studid still;
An' them teechurs sed, unannymus, ee'd a bin 'is cuntry's pride
If brane fever 'adn't takkl'd 'im three days before 'ee dide.

THE VETERAN'S TALE.

THE cuirassiers of Milhaud, with their long and curveless
    swords,
Charged on our decimated square, whilst Montbrun's Polish
    hordes
Hovered in clouds upon our flanks throughout the livelong day,
Spearing the helpless wounded and the dying as they lay ;
God save the King ! likewise the Queen ! that was a fight indeed,
But England's Trust was held by lads of English bulldog breed
From Lincoln and Northumbria, from Yorkshire's pleasant dales,
From southern downs, from Severn and the Marches of old
    Wales,
And in command was Picton, he, whose weakness for cold steel
Oft lent unto a Briton's gaze the flying Frenchman's heel.
Ours was the Fifth Division, sir, the " Fighting Fifth," whose
    fame
For trusting to the steel alone immortalized its name ;
'Fore God, we were but mortal men, and the dappled chargers
    foam,
Beflaked us with their Gallic hate, when Milhaud charged us
    home
And broke our square, where Drouet's storm of leaden hail had
    borne
Its tale of woe to English hearts—mere lads, though battle-worn ;
Yet closer round the colours we survivors grimly stood
To save them from the foeman's hand, or dye them with our
    blood ;
But in our dire extremity good comrades' help was near,
From British arms fell sabre cuts, from British throats a cheer ;
And when the day was won, at roll call, Picton twitted me,
" What ! Sergeant ! Frenchmen pierce the square, that such a
    thing should be."
Quoth I, saluting : " General, it's true they got in there,
But, thanks to British hearts and arms, they never *left* the
    square ! "

AT EVENTIDE.

IT was the pensive hour of Eventide,
   When the last beams the western hill tops greet,
And a loved sister lingered by my side,
   The waves of ocean murm'ring at our feet.

Calmly yon waters roll'd their silver flood,
   As we twain read at sunset's parting hour,
Sweet was the perfume of the opening bud,
   But oh! how fair to me the blossom'd flower.

And through glad seasons we were wont to roam,
   By the Nine Sisters' pathway, hand in hand,
Till Heav'n—weep not, my heart, had call'd her home,
   To the far mansions of the Better Land.

For they on whom the gods have smiled, die young,
   And short their travail in this vale of tears,
Not theirs the darkened hour when earth has flung
   Its solemn shadows o'er the coming years.

And I, way-worn by stress of weary years,
   Stand by Death's shore at Life's calm Eventide,
Soon we shall walk beyond this vale of tears,
   In the unclouded splendour—side by side.

FAREWELL.

All hail ! Princess ! from dear old England's strand,
  We welcomed thee to this our Western land,
Whose stalwart sons, in '13 bravely stood,
And served thy fathers' throne thro' fields of blood,
At Burlington, and glorious Lundy's Lane,
And Queenston Heights, where gallant Brock was slain,
With many a noble hero heart, whose name
Has deeply scored the classic roll of fame.
And farewell, thou most noble Lord of Lorne !
Whose kindly ways thy heritage adorn ;
As one endowed with ev'ry manly grace,
We welcomed thee, thou heir of Argyle's race ;
A race whose " feats of arms " so proudly stand
In records of old Scotia's heath-clad land ;
Farewell ! and should we never meet again,
May Father Time glance kindly o'er ye twain,
And lightly touch the Argyle ducal shrine,
Where England's Rose and Scotland's Thistle twine.

ANGEL EUSTACE.

*F*OR aye, on earth, is hush'd that baby-voice,
 —Sweet echo of a gentle mother's love—
But, welcome thought, bright angels now rejoice
 To hear those tones in the great choir above.

And we, who with sad tears his clay consign
 To mother-earth, would kiss the chastening rod
Of Him whose wisdom saw our loved resign
 A fair immortal soul unto its God.

VIOLET.

*T*HERE is mischief in your eye—little Vi! little Vi!
 There is danger in that bearing I am sure;
Though your looks be even saintly, yet language can but faintly
 Tell the diff'rence twixt your acts and looks demure;
For instance there's the baby;—you kiss him and, it may be,
 That you never thought to do that youngster any harm,
But oft his yells and flinching tell of surreptitious pinching
 And the impress of your fingers on his tender little arm.

And I think you often try—little Vi! little Vi!
 To be a mother, in your own peculiar way,
To dirty little Mollie—that fractured, one-eyed dolly
 Whom dearest auntie gave you on your natal day.
Oh! how you whack and spank her, and then politely thank her,
 As the humour takes, betimes, your little ladyship,
No wonder that to Mary, the milkman said he'd " nary
 Seed the hequal of 'er for a reg'lar little clip."

But I know of actions sly—little Vi !—little Vi !
  Towards the humble author of your presence on this earth,
Who in his peaceful study, oft ponders whether should he
  Be stern or laughter-loving at thy fascinating mirth.
How well does he remember yon night in calm September
  When you saw your active parent spring high into the air,
And you know such worldly rising, and the poet's agonizing
  Was the bent pin you had left within his study chair.

Yet when thou wert like to die—little Vi ! little Vi !
  He knows the weight of grief that lay upon each heart,
And turn'd the coming morrow into utter woe and sorrow
  For those who strove to stay the grim destroyer's art.
And when Death's bolt miscarried, and the angel's coming tarried,
  What joy within our walls when thy plaintive little cry
Told us the God of gladness had pity on our sadness,
  Had touched in peace thy garment, little Vi ! little Vi !

BABY CLARENCE.

Goo ! little man.   Long ago the whole household
  Has gladly acknowledged thy infantile sway,
And each flies at a nod from the youthful Bulgarian
  Whom the slaves of his will have short-coated to-day.
Bless his heart !   There he sits with his newly-clad honours,
  How he chuckles and crows with ineffable grace
As he coolly accepts the glad homage of vassals
  Who worship the dimples that star his young face.
By and by he'll wax weary of fussing and nonsense,
  For the drowsy-god woos when the long shadows creep ;
And it seems to us all like the angels in Heaven
  Is Clarence, our boy, as he smiles in his sleep.

ETHEL.

HY face anon demure, then wreath'd awhile
With honest girlhood's fascinating smile;
Thine unbent brow, thy rounded, dimpled chin,
And blood-red lips that curtain pearls within.
Ethel! thy kindly ways and features bear
The impress of a life divinely fair;
If sympathetic love towards distress
Can merit aught of human happiness,
If riches were of charity the meed,
Then hast thou wealth and happiness indeed.

TO A FRIEND.

HERISH and train, dear coz, with gentle hand,
The flowers of love that bind thy household band
In bonds of slavery, whose sweet restraint
Instinctive shrinks from Discord's blighting taint.
Methinks bright angels, from the realms above,
Gaze on and bless that beauteous household love
Which flings a glorious halo round the dome
And crowns the sacred edifice of home.

And when life's storms and pilgrimage are o'er,
When faintly looms the far-off golden shore,
And thy weak mortal frame and halting breath
Are merged within the gloomy shades of Death,
May watchful, tender-hearted friends be nigh,
To catch thy gentle spirit's parting sigh,
Loved ones who'll whisper low, as bowed in prayer,
" The life now fled was one serenely fair."

HEATON RISE.

AFAR I view with loving eyes
 The lovely lanes of Heaton-Rise.
'Tis there I see the Effra Road,
Where once the Effra River flowed,
Whose shaded banks, in times of yore,
Tribute unto fashion bore ;
'Tis there, I know, a lovelorn maid
Has passed from life when love decayed,
And he, who once was lover true,
Had left the old love for the new.

The Hill of Herne—like some sweet dream,
O'erthrows, as 'twere, a transient gleam
Of days gone by, when from his cell
The hermit heard the vesper bell.
His face I see, with unkempt hair,
And frame bowed down in silent prayer,
Whilst softly in the twilight dim
I hear the nuns' sweet Vesper Hymn.
 . . . . . .

Far, far away—beyond the sea—
These loved scenes lie, so dear to me,
Enshrined within my loving heart,
Their mem'ries never can depart.

THE SIGHING OF THE FIRS.

HARK! I hear the dark wind-singer, and the night-gloom gathers fast
As I linger at the casement, dreaming o'er the faded past ;
All those bright scenes unforgotten, I behold at such an hour
Days when Life seemed full of gladness—born of childhood's happy dower.
O, ye hours of careless boyhood, midst those scenes far, far away,
When the dawning of each morrow seemed more bright than yesterday !
And my heart is sad within me, and the tear of anguish blurs
As I listen in the gloaming to the Sighing of the Firs.

Where are all those byegone faces ? they whom I have loved and known ?
Do the sons of men still greet them ? or has nature claimed her own ?
Do they tread the paths of travail ? or do now their saintly eyes
Gaze in rapture, midst the ransomed, on the vales of paradise
Where are never tears nor sadness, where the storm-blast never lowers
O'er the white-robed ones whose vision is of other kind than ours ?
This the thought that steals upon me ; this the chord of sadness stirs,
As I listen in the gloaming to the Sighing of the Firs.

One—ere youth had passed to manhood, girded on his maiden sword—
Would ye know its crimson sheathing ? Seek the treacherous Afghan horde.
Some, I know, have reach'd the harbour, and the tears of kinship yield
Tribute to a martyr-hero, slain in Afric's mission field.

Distant Orient, Australasia, and the West Coast—each can tell
Of life's fitful fever ended, of the way-worn sleeping well,
And across the waste of waters calls one sweet voice—even *hers*
As I listen in the gloaming to the Sighing of the Firs.

From the peaceful halls of Silence, whence pale mortals shrink
    aghast,
Comes to me a vision saintly of the long departed past,
She, who through long years has slumbered 'neath a cloister'd
    southern pile,
Surely I can hear those accents, surely view that pensive smile.
Take me, gentlest, best of Mothers, lead me once more by the
    hand
As in childhood's days you led me—nearer to the better land;
Oh, it may be idle dreaming, and mayhap fond fancy errs,
Yet I catch one glimpse of Heaven in the Sighing of the Firs.

LITTLE GRETCHEN.

PLUMP, demure-faced little Gretchen !
    In yon Swabian cottage rude,
Where her sire, the Landgraf's woodman,
    Dwells in rustic solitude.

And the little maiden, sadly,
    Near her grandam takes her stand,
But I must confess that Gretchen
    Recks not of "the better land."

Of whose glory old Katrina's
    Soul doth inwardly rejoice,
As she reads unto the maiden
    In her crack'd old German voice.

Ah! I trow that little Gretchen's
  Childish thoughts are far away
'Midst the pine trees of the Northland,
  Whence comes Santa Claus—they say.

I don't blame thee, old Katrina,
  Nor the maiden at thy side,
Thou art very near "the border,"
  As for her—'tis Christmas-tide.

And I sympathize with Gretchen,
  And Katrina, too, because
What is Christmas-tide to children
  If they don't have Santa Claus?

What is life unto Katrina
  If her poor old palsied hand
May not clasp the letter'd story
  Of dear Heaven—her Promised Land!

————

THE RED HAND OF O'NEIL.

BRIGHT gleams the fair sunlight where blue laughing waters
    The shores of Iernis at morning-tide lave,
Emblaz'ning in splendour the vessels of Scota
    That breast the broad bosom of Inbher Sceine's wave.
All regal the air of the mother-queen Scota,
    With her sable-decked brow, and her silver-white hair;
All stately her bearing as, fronting her chiefmen,
    Her accents ring out on the calm summer air:

" In the splendour of sunlight, ye sons of far Scythia,
  Yon emerald valleys stretch fair from this bay,
Then say ye, my Scythians, choose, which of my offspring
  Shall o'er them the sceptre of royalty sway?
Eber Find, primal pledge of my good lord Milesius,
  Oft has crimsoned the field with his dead father's brand,
And Ermon Niul bears the soul of a hero ;
  Choose! Which of my offspring shall reign in the land? "

She ceases. And loudly the voice of contention
  Is heard in the midst of her warrior band,
And some will that Eber, the beetle browed Eber,
  Shall reign as their king in this fair Western land ;
But others, who love the bright face of the last born,
  And have secretly chafed beneath Eber Find's frown,
Say that none save the younger, the open-browed Ermon,
  Shall wield the fair sceptre, or wear the bright crown.

Then are heard o'er their clamour, the words of Queen Scota,
  " Be still d in our presence Dissension's harsh voice,
'Twixt Eber and Ermon shall be the vex'd question,
  Since my faithful and true are divided in choice.
Give Eber a linter, and with it two rowers,
  Give Ermon the same, not a follower more,
All arm'd as for war, let them row from our vessel,
  And the land shall be his who first touches the shore.

" Go forth, then, my sons! " Half defiant is Eber,
  As he and his rowers descend the ship's side ;
And the partisan cries vex the calm summer ether
  As the boats of the twain lay abreast on the tide ;
But all changed is the face of the once smiling Ermon,
  An expression so stern never dwelt there before ;
And he deigns not a glance, for the bent of his vision
  Is changelessly fixed on the far away shore.

Away! They are gone! Strain each limb, swarthy rowers,
    Till your eyeballs nigh leap·from their dark caverned space!
Pull! pull! till the swelled vein is strained unto bursting,
    For a dynasty waits for the first in this race.
And the rent wave is spurned by the four mighty rowers,
    As the boats near the land 'neath their swift maddened reach,
And the Queen-mother watches afar, for the moment
    Which beholds the first Scythian on Inbher Sceine's beach.

Oh! why lags his boat, but a moment since foremost?
    Why yon swift stream of crimson that spouts with each.breath?
'Tis Ermon's best oar in convulsive distortion,
    As he flings up his arms in the pallor of death.
Oh! more bitter than death, in the moment of victory,
    To have torn from his grasp the fair meed of renown,
To see Eber erect, with a gesture of triumph,
    For the leap that shall bring him a kingdom and crown.

But, swift as a flash, from the gloom of its sheathing
    Leaps to glittering life now the younger son's brand,
Through flesh, bone and sinew its keen edge goes crashing,
    And Ermon is lacking his sinister hand;
From the might of his right arm, in rapid expulsion,
    The shorn limb whirls shoreward, fast spurting its gore,
" And mine is the crown and the sceptre," gasps Ermon,
    " Since mine is the hand that first touches its shore."

And the sceptre was his. But the generous Ermon
    Shared with Eber the lands that pertained to his throne;
And Ermon and Eber, o'er the vales of Iernis,
    Were crowned as twin king on the Destiny Stone.
And down through the ages, the O'Neils of old Erin
    Tell with pride of brave Ermon, whose merciless steel
Hurled defeat into triumph, on Inbher Sceine's billow,
    And gave to their arms the Red Hand of O'Neil.

EPITAPH ON AN EARLY SETTLER.

Pause, pilgrim footsteps! rev'rently draw near,
  The vanguard of a nation slumbers here.

Mayhap he wander'd once by Yarrow's side,
Or dreamed where Severn rolls its volumed tide.

Perchance his infant gaze first saw the light
Nigh lordly Snowdon's heaven-ambitioned height.

Or thrilled his boyish heart, in bygone days,
At sound of stricken Erin's mournful lays.

Amid the crowded marts of Old World strife,
He yearned to breathe a purer, freer life.

Brave heart! Beyond Atlantic's sullen roar
He sought a home on this wild western shore.

His stalwart might and keen, unerring aim,
Taught lurking savages to dread his name.

In peril's midst he raised his cabin rude,
And lived—his one companion, solitude.

Yet not his only one. Where'er he trod,
In simple childlike faith he walked with God.

With quenchless courage and unflinching toil,
Redeemed he day by day the unwilling soil.

Primeval gloom, beneath his sturdy blows,
Beam'd forth in glebes that blossomed as the rose.

And years rolled by.   Europe her exiles sent,
Around him grew a thriving settlement.

Yet, 'tis not good for man to live alone,
He wooed and won a maiden for his own.

The flowers of June smiled on his marriage kiss,
And thrice ten years he tasted wedded bliss.

His children, born 'neath Freedom's own roof-tree,
Were cradled in the arms of Liberty.

They lived to bless the author of their birth,
And by their deeds renew'd his honest worth.

His neighbours loved the kindly, upright way,
Of one whose yea was yea, whose nay was nay.

And, did dispute arise, his word alone
Was jury, judge and verdict blent in one.

Dark day which saw, and gloomier hearts which said,
" The father of the settlement is dead ; "

When full of years, beloved on ev'ry hand,
His spirit left them for the Better Land.

Tread softly, stranger ! rev'rently draw near,
The vanguard of a nation slumbers here.

THE TRAMP.

Scion of Ishmael's outcast race, he traverses the land
  From broad Atlantic's granite cliffs to blue Pacific's strand,
The frozen north has gazed on him, and southern winds have
    played
Around his uncombed shaggy locks beneath the mango's shade.
Of conscience only innocent he winds his tortuous way,
And rifled hen-roosts, plundered barns, yield tribute to his sway.
Seek ye a godless rascal, an unmitigated scamp ?
Ho ! self-sufficient vagabond—Hail ! soap-despising Tramp.

His linen is not pure—in fact, it harbours more than the
Hop-skip-and-jumping vagaries of the gently-nurtured flea ;
His boots (one " Wellington," the other nondescript) are shorn
With tender care in little slits that ease the venomed corn ;
Button and brace are nought to him except as old wives' tales :
Stout bits of twine are all he asks, secured by honoured nails ;
And a good thick stick, for legends such as *cave canem* cramp
The mis-directed genius of the philosophic Tramp.

His fighting pulse beats normally when manhood bars the way,
But if 'tis only petticoats then changed's the time o' day ;
No bully in Alsatian haunts when " vapouring the huff,"
Equalled his frothy violence, or spake in tones more gruff.
But there are modern Joans of Arc who make a plucky stand
With Household Honour in their hearts, and a "shooter" in
    each hand ;
And then 'tis laughable to watch that troubadour decamp
With the injured feelings of a much deluded Tramp.

Churches he views with some respect—from taxes they're
    exempt ;
But for work or aught like cleanliness he's the loftiest contempt.
The civil courts are 'neath contempt, bum-bailiffs unknown ills ;

He ne'er receives a morning call for unpaid tradesmen's bills.
His blinking eyes with tears for human kind are never dim ;
His griefs are little unto men, far less are theirs to him.
If nonchalance for others' woes be the true patrician stamp
There's none can " down " that nobleman, the free and easy
Tramp.

Confused ideas of *mine* and *thine* lodge him in durance vile ;
When freedom dawns, and spring's not here, what's he to do
meanwhile ?
He solves the problem in a trice—joins the Temperance cause
As a " terrible example " of Dame Nature's outraged laws.
This keeps him like a fighting-cock, but the moment winter's gone,
He skips from grace with all that he can lay his clutches on,
And anger reigns when it is known in Prohibition's camp ;
" 'Evin 'elps the chap wot 'elps hisself " 's the motto of a Tramp.

Yet sneer not lightly at him, friends, while we through torrid days
Burn life's short candle at each end, he strolls by pleasant ways;
Whilst we with noses at the grindstone slave, his mid-day dream,
Pulses beneath umbrageous shades hard by some babbling
stream.
What tho' we rest on feathered couch when night dews kiss the
day—
'Tis just as clean and cooler far to snore on new-mown hay.
Oh ! could we have our morning tub, our night-cap free from
damp,
We'd change with thee, O Scallawag ! we would, illustrious
Tramp.

TORONTO'S GLORIOUS DEAD.

IN MEMORIAM, LIEUT. FITCH, WHO DIED ON THE FIELD OF HONOUR.

TOLL ! sad-voiced bells, a dirge of woe. To his last narrow bed
 Far Occident returns to-day Toronto's honoured dead ;
Not *with* his shield, but *on* it borne, comes he who scorned all
 fear,
And the pathos of a nation's grief bedews his blood-stained bier.
Yea, halo'd Vict'ry shades her light in patriotic gloom
For him, the leal-hearted youth, who sought a soldier's tomb—
Peal slow, ye bells, your solemn notes o'er his devoted head,
Far Occident returns to-day Toronto's honoured dead.

When desolating war's alarm rang through the startled land,
When loud the midnight cry " To arms " was heard on ev'ry
 hand.
Ready ! aye ready ! gallant Fitch, for tented field or fray.
Nobly and well the trust's redeem'd reposed in him that day,
On far Batoche's stricken field his life he freely gave—
To-day *we* give—'tis all we can—a soldier's honoured grave ;
And street and square vibrate beneath the serried column's tread,
For Occident returns to-day Toronto's noble dead.

Sleep on, O gallant heart ! sleep on. For thee all strife is done,
The bloody marge of battle pass'd, the leaves of cypress won ;
What tho' the rattling fusillade has closed the mournful scene,
The loyal heart of Canada shall keep thy memory green ;
And grey-haired sires, in years unborn, shall tell of childhood's
 day,
And unto wond'ring childhood's ears, and reverent hearts shall
 say,
Peace with *true Honour* crown'd the land, a beauteous lustre
 shed,
When Occident returned in state Toronto's glorious dead.

THESE DEGENERATE MODERN DAYS.

GLIBLY fall the tones regretful o'er the pleasant times no more,
  When this earth of ours was younger, in the goodly days of
      yore ;
When full dress was but a fig leaf in the pre-historic times ;
When the troubadour and jongleur sang in mediæval rhymes ;
When fat Hal, our kingly Bluebeard —model of false-hearted-
      ness—
Changed his wives almost as often as he changed his royal dress ;
And those days of England's Georges—mention of them is to
      praise
With a parting sigh and sneer at these degenerate modern days.

In the good days pre-historic folks camped out in goat-hair tents,
Innocent of baths, etcetera, scorning " house " advertisements ;
Eastern night-dews picnic'd round them, and our Aryan forbear's
      phiz
Grimaced as its owner wallowed in the pangs of "rheumatiz."
'Neath *our* roof-trees we may never sleep in soul-entrancing joy,
With a billy-goat beside us, like the patriarchal boy.
Sheltered by our bricks and mortar, winter's frosts and summer's
      rays
Are, alas ! but little felt in these degenerate modern days.

In the mediæval period murder, violence and lust
Made things rosy for those mashers who are with the saints, we
      trust ;
Happy, happy mediævals ! when crusading was the rage,
Home returned ye, wives re-married ; nothing left but lonely age.
We in peace and safety slumber in our household's calm retreat,
And our lullaby's the tramping of Muldoony on his beat—
That is, if he isn't " vittling " 'neath our cook's admiring gaze
(For "the finest" dote on cooks in these degenerate modern days).

In the reign of bluff King Harry swells but seldom died in bed,
For the bloated Tudor's weakness was a loving subject's head ;
And full many a noble victim of that same despotic power
Passed beneath the traitor's gateway to the headsman of the
 tower.
Nowadays our English monarchs trouble not their royal heads
As to whether loyal subjects die in ditches or in beds.
All they ask is peace and plenty, with the right to pleasant ways ;
And this whim we always grant in these degenerate modern days.

When that bright quartette, " the Georges " figured at the royal
 helm,
Dinners were but drunken orgies 'mongst the gentry of the realm;
And —to tell the truth—the parson gambled, swore and drank his
 fill,
Called his man out, yea, and winged him with the heartiest good-
 will.
Now the exile of Oporto, and the tear of champagne's vine
Are exchanged for *aqua pura* (Anglicé: old Adam's wine) ;
And *our* parson—Heaven bless him !—for deliverance he prays
From liquor, crime and sudden death in these degenerate modern
 days.

Still we hear the tones regretful for the goodly times no more,
Still that sentimental slobbering for the brave old days of yore.
And sometimes we can't help thinking, while folks of the bygone
 dream,
Of the comforts we're enjoying in these sneered-at days of steam.
Julius Cæsar was a hero, yet his came-saw-conquered tone
Never warbled " Thank you, Central ! " through the wondrous
 telephone.
Praise your past ! though haif its glory is but an exploded craze,
Still my vote and influence go for these degenerate modern days.

THE DEATH BED OF LOUIS XI.

ox of Valois! tell to the world what powers avails thee now!
Death's icy touch is on thy heart, his dews are on thy brow.

Whence comes the hue of mortal dread that pales thy withered
cheek?
Has sleeping conscience waked at last? Speak, sceptred mon-
ster, speak!

When fell thy victims' parting groans, coldly impassive thou;
The scene has chang'd; what sayest, then, O dying tyrant,
now?

Death, through long years thy vassal slave, is lord o'er thee at
last,
And 'midst his train of horrors troop the shadows of the past.

La Balue comes from living death, from Loche's circled fate,
Terror has stayed where mercy failed—long years of venomed
hate;

Guienne, fair offspring of thy royal mother's womb,
Points his dead hand at thee, O king! from his unhallow'd tomb.

Unshriven he died. Men thought him sped by fell disease
undone;
What of the secret chalice and the Abbot of St. John?

At yonder feast was the mad jester's tale denied,
Heir of the sainted Capet's throne, illustrious fratricide?

Ha! see'st yon spectral form that gibbers from the outer gloom,
Swathed in the garb of St. Denis—the odours of the tomb?

Fling back the arras* wider still. Rememb'rest thou that glance,
When he was the Most Christian King, and thou a Child of
     France?

Ay! leprous soul! 'tis he—thy sire; his pilgrimage below
Shortened by thee, his son—his son, yet most relentless foe.

When pealed the tocsin's hateful call to foul seditious strife,
Who raised the standard of revolt against a father's life?

Who, pardoned by a father's love revived the Praguerie?
What skills to ask thee who: thy dastard heart impeacheth thee.

Beneath yon grey embattled walls there sleeps, till doom,
     beguiled,
Armagnac's ill-starred consort and her butchered unborn child.

Lectour!   No darker tale than thine on history's tarnished page;
A ravished truce, a poisoned cup, and a king's insatiate rage.

And one with blood-stained mitre lends this hour a crimson hue,
Whose solemn accents brand thee with the hireling Flemish
     crew.

Bourbon, Prince Bishop of Liége, loved prelate of " The Bold,"
Lays his dark murder at the door of Louis' secret gold.

Hark! Blending with the voice of prayer, and the chapel
     organ's tones,
There comes from 'neath these very walls the wail of captive
     groans.

There, hopeless ones in gloom still pass their nigh forgotten
     lives.
(Peace! suffering hearts! a despot's death shall rend your rust-
     ing gyves).

Throne of thy sire, well served in love, thine by mean slavish
    fear,
His service won by kingly smiles, *thine* by the orphan's tear.

Toward dark Plessis' terrace plies no more the homeward wing,
For tears and blood hold daily tryst in the garden of the king.

Foul carrion throng the royal chase, where voice of song is mute
(Rare haunt for carrion where each bough bears hideous *human*
    fruit).

Mumble thy prayers to Her of Clery now; call loud to her;
E'en she, thy patroness, is deaf to-night, O whited sepulchre!

Craven! there is no peace. Unheeded now each frenzied call;
A greater tyrant e'en than thou holds thy black heart in thrall.

Fainter and fainter fall thy shrieks beneath the avenging rod;
Son of Valois! France leaves thee here to conscience and thy
    God.

---

* Hallam *(History of the Middle Ages,* chap. ix., part 2,) has implied a
doubt whether great houses were furnished with hangings so soon as the latter
part of the fifteenth century. The weight of evidence, however, is strongly
against this historian, for the narrative of the *Lord of Grauthuse* specifies the
hangings of cloth of gold in the apartments in which that lord was received
by our own King Edward the Fourth -a cotemporary of Louis XI.,—also the
hangings of white silk and linen in the chamber appropriated to himself at
Windsor. Again, long before this period (not to mention the Bayeux
Tapestry), viz., in the reign of the third Edward (1344) a writ was issued to
inquire into the mystery of working tapestry; and in 1398 the celebrated
arras hangings at Warwick Castle are mentioned.

JACK TARTAR.

Jack Tartar was a British salt, deserter from his ship,
    Before him frown'd the jungle's gloom, behind—the bosun's
      whip !
Was Jack disheartened ? Not a bit of it, though twelve rupees
And a roll of Limerick twist comprised his earthly wealth ; yet
    these,
Combined with native impudence, brought him, at last, before
The scimitars and tulwars of Baroda's Guicowar.
And just in time to hear the Gèkwar's proclamation read,
Offering one-quarter lak for a decapitated head
Whose blood-stained fangs and tongue had torn and lapp'd the
    crimson tide
Of life from human veins.

               " Why, blow my heyes ! I'll 'ave 'is 'ide."
Quoth Jack, " If I goes back, I gets five score, or wuss, trust
    'em for that ;
I'd better *face* them tiger claws than *back* the bosun's cat."
No sooner said than done. His dwindling wealth secured a
    gun,
Knife, ammunition, and a shikaree. Ere set of sun,
Bold Jack, accompanied by his guide, had sought the jungle's
    gloom
For weal or woe—wealth, or a tiger's stomach for his tomb.
Rare luck was his—sailor's proverbial luck—on the next day
They stood beside a running stream, and the Bengal stood at
    bay.
Flash ! Bang ! A hideous roar—and Jack—oh ! where was he ?
Weep not ! That nimble strategist had scaled a friendly tree
In the liveliest style ; in time, and only just in time, to see
The stricken beast make collops of his shikaree.
But who may e'er resist his fate. Kismet ! another roar !—

Clawing, and tearing at the earth, and the striped one was no
　　more.
Jack clambered down, sliced off his dead foe's head, scooped out
　　a hole
For his dead guide, and made a bee-line for the Gèkwar's dole.
Baroda reached, a native wine-shop met his thirsting view;
To see it was to enter.

　　　　　　　　　　　　　　Amid the motley crew
Assembled there, was one*—a Parsee bhèestie-wallah, in whose
　　eyes
The baleful spark of envy gleamed at sight of Jack's rich prize.
" By Zarathustra's source of light " thus thought that low
　　Parsee,
" And shall such dazzling wealth enrich so vile a one as he ?
Nay ! by the sacred Zend Avesta ! it must, it shall not be,
But one shall have this great reward, and that same one is *me.*"
Accosting Jack, this trickster asked him if he didn't think
His " innards " would be none the worse for the matter of a
　　drink.
Nor was Jack loath ; glass after glass of arrack Tartar quaff'd,
And when the fiery draught had done its work, his tempter
　　laugh'd,
Snatched up the tiger's head unseen, nor was it long before
His form was cringing in the presence of the Guicowar.
A craven cur, the Gèkwar thought, and then aloud he said,
" *You* killed this beast ? "—" Iss, Sahib." " And *you* cut off his
　　head ? "
Salaam ! " Iss, Sahib." Yet still the Gèkwar was possessed with
　　doubt.
" Approach ! Dost see this gray hair in my beard ?—well pluck
　　it out."
The craven moved with trembling hand, to snatch it from its
　　mates,
When snap ! the Rajah made a bite at him. As if the Fates
Were fronting him, the Parsee backward leapt, in wild affright.

" A jackal cur," the Gèkwar cried " Bah ! put him out of sight ! "
A motion of his hand. Guards ! Scimitars !—one slashing blow,
And out o' window fired—a head rolled in the square below.

 . . . .

Anon the dwaling mists of drunken stupor rolled away,
And Jack arose.

     And then there was the very deuce to pay.
In five short minutes after he had miss'd that tiger's head,
He'd cleared the whole shebang, and left the landlord there for
  dead ;
Then, bull-dog like, renewed the fight outside, and many felt
The qualmishness of lusty thumps delivered neath the belt.
A punkah-wallah *fann'd* his ire, and felt the sad surprise
Occasioned by a British fist applied between the eyes.
A passing Brahmin, who had interfered to quell the row,
Fell gasping, with the brand of *self-defence* upon his brow ;
And when a pious Mussul hinted at the drunkard's doom,
Jack swept the pavement in a jiff, and that Mussul was his broom,
And the atmosphere was blue with oaths, and Asiatic d--ns
That fell from the proprietors of shattered diaphragms.
Ah me ! it was a battered-up procession, when, at last,
By force of numbers only, they had bound Jack Tartar fast,
And led him to the Presence.

     " Loosen his bonds," the Gèkwar cried,
" And what dost here ? "—" I wants my pay," undaunted Jack
  replied,
" For killing that 'ere cat wot's eated up so many men."
" *You* killed the man-eater ? "—" In course I did, my buck, and
  w'en
I snickers horf 'is 'ed, I steers for 'ere to get my pay,
But, blow me tight ! some swab 'as cribbed the tom-cat's nob
  away."
" His looks are honest, tho' his speech is free." the Gèkwar said,

" We'll try his courage as we did the other's." But instead
Of testing Tartar's nerve himself, the wily Guicowar
Made much detested Ramsetjee, Jack's interlocutor.
Now Ramatoola Ramsetjee, a pompous card was he,
And stout, so stout, his fatness was a sight for saints to see.
" Approach me, child of Frangistan ! " † in haughtiest tones he
    cried,
And in a second (rather less) the *child* was at his side.
" Dost see this gray hair in my beard ? "—" I does."—" Well !
    pluck it out."
" In course I will, my hearty," and a most unusual shout
Of laughter rose, when Ramatoola, with an elephantine roar,
Snapp'd at Jack's hand in imitation of the Guicowar ;
But ere he could repeat the dose, Jack had him in a trice,
Yea ! had his head in chancery, as tho' 'twere in a vice.
And how the Rajah yell'd and laugh'd on that eventful day,
And burst his collar-button when he heard Jack Tartar say,
As he smote poor Rammy's left jaw, and banged him on the
    right,
" Ha ! would yer, would yer bite ? Aha ! ye fat thief, would
    yer bite ? "

.   .   .   .

For years, on the Vindayhan hills, fear check'd each childish
    game,
When bandit sires but whispered of Jack Tartar's dreaded name,
And the terrors of invasion vex'd the Gèkwar's heart no more
When Tartar ruled the province as his Minister of War.

---

   * The author has taken a slight liberty with the probabilities in making a
Parsee descend to the humble condition of a water carrier.

   † "Child of Frangistan "—an expression more common to the Moham-
medan than the Hindu, but may not Ramsetgee have had a weakness for an
"outside" phrase, just as many of our own friends who, not by any means
saturated with the classics, dearly love to lard their conversation with quotations from the Latin phrases found at the end of every modern dictionary ?

THE OLD COACHING INN.

A Y ! it stands, and has stood for a century or more,
    And its signboard still creaks by the black oaken door,
But the lion and legend have faded at last,
'Neath the hot breath of June, and December's chill blast.
Yet a form may be spied in the broad light of day,
Though all but the outline has long passed away,
And left but a ghost there to mourn for the din
Once heard 'neath the roof of the old Coaching Inn.

How welcome its cheer when the herald of morn
Was borne on the notes of the guard's bugle horn ;
What a bustle was there, and a hurrying forth
When the Royal Mail coach rumbled up from the north,
And the dew-stricken " outsides," bedraggled and chilled,
At the great kitchen fire felt their shiverings stilled,
And the guard passed the news o'er his noggin o' gin
While the cattle were changed at the old Coaching Inn.

O ruddy crowned hearth ! where the wayfarer might
Forget in thy sunshine the moorland's despite ;
How those rafters have echoed the jest and the song
When the crown bowl of punch made the even' less long ;
What chuckles were heard when the stranger guest told
How the Knights of the road " eased " the Bishop of old,
And a time-serving roar shook the fat double chin
That belonged to mine host of the old Coaching Inn !

Then a silence fell on that assembly awhile,
And mine host's mottled face wore a curious smile,
And the cobbler laughed out as he bade them good eve,
Whilst the " score "-burden'd tailor grinned low in his sleeve ;

For 'twas more than suspected by those who knew best
That the sire of mine host on his death-bed confessed
That the Church's despoilers were more than akin
To the landlord and son of the old Coaching Inn.

But stilled are the notes of the cheery-faced guard,
And mine host sleepeth well in the village church yard,
The cobbler's rude laughter is hushed evermore,
And the rats scurry past o'er the once sanded floor.
Alas! and alack for the days that are gone,
Alas! for that hostel deserted and lone,
Alas! for this tribute—nor deem it a sin—
A sigh and good-bye to the old Coaching Inn.

THE PIC-NIC BOY.

THE Sunday school young pic-nic boy is on the war path now
    With malice prepense in his heart, defiance on his brow;
We know, yes, well we know he is, alack-a-day! alas!
We found it out the other day when sitting on the grass,
With raptured thoughts of heaven-born bliss, and hearts sur-
    charg'd with mirth,
And not a single thought betwixt ourselves and mother earth,
As suddenly we rose and found, with sad and angry hearts,
By that cub's undermining tricks we'd squashed a plate of
    tarts;
And when we turned to drown our grief, we found at once
    that he
Had placed a pinch of horrid salt in each one's cup of tea;
Remarking in his low, profane, exasperating way,
About our looking "bully cheap," and "how's yer purp to-day?"
We "ran to catch him ere he fell," but only tore our clothes,
Whilst he had skipped behind a tree, his finger at his nose.

But punishment o'ertaketh guilt, and has done since the Fall,
" The mills of gods grind slowly, but they grind exceeding small,"
And this young, rising, Christian lad, who goes to Sunday school,
Is no—sweet heaven be praised and thanked—exception to the
 rule ;
For, shortly after, prowling round amidst some stumps of trees,
He poked and stirr'd 'midst other things, a nest of bumble-bees,
Oh ! what an active Band of Hope he suddenly became !
Such howling, acrobatic feats would add to Barnum's fame ;
He rubb'd, and scratch'd, and raced around, a sort of " as you
 please,"
Whilst, putting in a pile of work, those pious busy bees
Rebuked in sharp and stinging terms that low, blaspheming lad,
Whose sentiments were more than strong, and less refined than
 sad.
O ! kindly fates, who cursed us with the school-boy's baneful glee,
Yet blessed us with its antidote—the gentle bumble-bee !

OLD PUFF.

His back was up, when first we met ; his tail as big as six ;
 Two mongrel curs were worrying him, but vigorous, soulful
 kicks
Well placed on unregenerate parts, left Puss and I alone,
And in that hour of victory Old Puff became mine own.
My little heart went out to him ; how often did I steal
A march on cook's well stored domain—ere he should lack a
 meal ;
And what a proud young cub I was, when that brown Norwgian
 rat
Was slain in single combat by Old Puff, my Thomas Cat.

How dignified his solemn mien when shadow'd hours had fled,
What halos wreath'd his pure, young face whilst morning prayers
 were said ;

And, when each sought those daily tasks which wait on duty's
    call,
His Nibbs would seek a sun-bath'd ledge that flank'd the garden
    wall ;
And how the dogs would yelp at him, and gnash their watering
    teeth
In raging impotence ; whilst, gazing on his foes beneath—
Serene and calm, because secure, too truly great to spat,
There beam'd the non-committal phiz of Puff, my Thomas Cat.

Fie ! fie ! that decorous cats should shun the narrow path of
    right ;
Old Puff began to put on airs and stay out late at night.
I reason'd gently with him, for our old time friendship's sake,
Then firmly.   It was all in vain—Puff was a hopeless rake.
But Patience rules with feeble sway, where love is all unknown ;
Soon household tongues began to growl in no uncertain tone,
And hint about much broken sleep, and caterwauling chat,
For which they blamed the amorous lungs of Puff, my Thomas
    Cat.

Alas ! a dire complaint seized Puff, most strangely chang'd he
    grew,
And gradually grew worse before my sympathizing view.
I treated him for various ills, then thoroughly and well
Dosed him each day—oh, fruitless task—with pills of calomel ;
Oh ! bless my youthful innocence, and cuss feline deceit,
That such a sight as did one morn my wondering senses meet—
Five pretty kittens mewing there—blind as the fabled bat,—
And their shameless mother was Old Puff, mine erstwhile
    Thomas Cat.

THE COUNTY STEEPLECHASE.

OLD Bayard dead ? Ah ! how that name brings back a glorious time,
When existence seem'd a poem, and my life a happy rhyme.
Wild leaps my very heart's blood at the mention of yon day
When I, a stripling, mounted him—a handsome compact bay,
His blood three-quarters warm, and blood is bound to tell,
Strong in the withers, well ribb'd up ; his limbs ? sound as a bell,
And fit to run, though life itself were staked upon the race,
That day I cross'd the hog-skin in the County Steeplechase.

Nigh all the county swells were there. Stern Busfeild of the Grange
(The sceptred line may rise and fall—" ye Busfeilds nevvre cheynge "),
The Ayscough Yorkes, old Jack Stonehenge, the Master, from St. Ives,
With Lady Vi—the sweetest hostess, and the best of wives,
And one, oh ! such is love, pass'd by in calm patrician pride,
Unconscious of me as I chatted by the squire's side ;
And Cain's foul brand was near my heart, as, from her winsome face
Shot witching smiles on Reggie Vyne, my rival in love's race.

Sweet Audrey Leigh ! a subtle charm, a nameless beauty thine,
Within the temple of thy life the Graces held their shrine, ·
To Vyne—to me—thy bearing seem'd calm friendship—nothing more,
Nor glance, nor tone, a preference to either lover bore,
If Reggie proudly took the *pas* at morning rides, or calls,
I held the fort when ev'ning's ray had flush'd the western walls ;
If, when the tall elms lent their shade, Vyne was the lingering swain,
I shared with thee the moonlit hour that blanch'd the oriel pane.

Hark back! The race. "Open to all." Five pounds allow'd
    by·jocks,
The largest field I'd ever seen—'midst others (shade of Knox)
The Presbyterian, Papist, and—but why jot down the list
Of cracks which fretted for the word, 'neath spur and bridle-
    wrist ;
I fear'd but one, a chestnut mare, her rider—Reggie Vyne—
A blaze of hatred from his eyes, a glance of scorn from mine—
Hate, bitter hatred, moved our hearts : Hush ! Shame ! forget
    not now
The red Soudan, his foe-stain'd sword, and Reggie's lead-torn
    brow.

Three false breaks, and the flag went down—a splendid start—
    they said
" A sheet might cover all the lot." At first, I lost my head
Then settled calm possessed my nerves as Fagan forc'd the pace,
But first to lead is often last, at the finish of a race
And the Irishman, too eager, rose the colt a shade too fast,
Poor Shamrock ! t'was his maiden race—by Heav'ns ! 'twas his
    last—
Too low his jump, both forelegs smash'd, and Fagan left for
    dead,
As Vyne, and I, shot past—the chestnut leading by a head.

The Dustman made strong running next across the level plain,
But the pace too hot, brought the gelding back to his field again,
Now, bunched together on the sward, now, side by side, we
    spurr'd
Straight at the water-jump, and then " Spread eagle " was the
    word,
Splash ! Splash ! went half a score, 'midst laughter close allied
    to tears.
And the voice of many waters sang loud in *divers* ears,
And many a stately hunting hat from muddy horror rose
Like to a concertina when the latter's in repose.

The red-beck saw The Warbler and Mayflower come to grief;
A rasper bowl'd out Sunshine, and the filly Maple Leaf,
Sappho and Phaon broke their hearts in unavailing toil,
Hopeless the gap that fill'd their lungs with dust from Aberfoyle.
Old Cyclone found his Waterloo, as also Chanticleer,
In flound'ring through the heavy soil, where clay lands woo the mere,
And Charlie Drew, on Primrose, came an awful cropper, which
Left stumbling Primrose riderless, and Charlie in the ditch.

No thought for helpless Friendship's woe, a hurried, lightning glance
Shew'd me the field was beaten and the chestnut in advance;
But Bayard's blood was up and (no time was this to spare the steel)
Flew like an arrow to the front, at the pressure of my heel,
Aye! till we saw the bullfinch frown athwart the level mead,
He gave the mare a burster there, that taxed her utmost speed,
And then I nurs'd him for awhile, and smil'd as Vyne went past,
Leaving a cozy passage for me where the brambles crash'd.

He led at the fences and rails, oh grandly he took them all,
But Fear is known to Valour, and the mare refused the wall;
Thrice Vyne essayed to make the leap, thrice was he held in check,
"Pounded, by Jove! at last," I thought—and slashing Bayard's neck,
The crimson dripping from his flanks, I rush'd him at the wall;
Oh, heavens! he rear'd, and backward slipp'd—borne with him in the fall,
A thousand stars flashed on my eyes—my side was rack'd with pain,
But in a moment I was up and in my seat again.

Easier to bear a shatter'd rib, than brook yon sneering smile,
Worn by my rival as he topped the stone in gallant style,
Up! Up! and On! were the pale horse and rider both ahead,
Nobly the masonry was cleared, and Bayard onward sped ;
Sped on! the chestnut's quarter passed; sped on! lock'd level
    now,
Spurn'd was the furrowed line that mark'd the progress of the
    plough,
On! swept the chestnut! On! the bay! steel gored and flaked
    with foam ;
Pass'd, pass'd, the wattle, brook, and then we flogg'd and
    spurr'd for home.

Dead level up the straight we raced. Flog as he would, the bay,
A trifle dickey from his fall, was there and bound to stay.
On! On! we came, a wave of hats!—a hurricane of cheers,
Mad offspring of a thousand lungs, assail'd our startled ears,
And, nerved afresh, my noble horse, Bayard in name and deed,
Nerv'd him to show the crowd that last terrific burst of speed,
And one great shout, one awful yell, which might have roused
    the dead,
Told me the mare was beaten, and the bay had won by a head.

Cheerily rang the Master's voice, as he grasp'd my dexter hand,
And how they cheer'd brave Bayard, as we paced before " the
    stand."
" Handsomely ridden, my own dear boy," was all the old squire
    said,
But never a word or glance had I—save for one shapely head,
Nor gave my shatter'd ribs a thought, until I swerv'd and fell ;
But, ere I swoon'd, oh heart of mine, can words thy rapture tell ?
For by yon glance, yon love-lit glance, that flush'd her lovely
    face,
I had won, I *knew*, a dearer prize than the County Steeplechase.

BEREAVED.

A silent household mine.   Unbroken gloom
  Where once was mirth and childhood's glad surprise,
Ere yet the tear-dewed pathway of the tomb
  Had led unto the gates of Paradise.

Can I forget that hour when they had borne
  My one ewe lamb forth from the parent fold,
When bolt and bar closed on a heart forlorn,
  And left my little one out in the cold ?

Oft in my spirit's hour of dark unrest
  I seek one hallowed room with softened tread,
And, as the shadows lengthen from the west,
  Keep sacred tryst with relics of my dead.

Two little socks, his christening robe, a tress
  Of golden hair, and love-crown'd bassinette,
Once emblems of a mother's happiness,
  Ye shrine till death a stricken heart's regret.

I hear them whisper Murder's hideous name—
  A daughter of the hamlet, wooed in lust,
That, flamed with the madness of an open shame,
  Slew the frail offspring of illicit trust.

Deeply my sorrowing heart bemoans its fate,
  And murmurs at the chastening Hand which gave
To her a pledge of shame, a child of hate,
  And unto me, alas ! a little grave.

KILLED IN THE STRAIGHT.

ONLY a jockey awaiting the solemn Hereafter ;
    Only a crush'd form lay bleeding, inanimate there,
Uncheck'd for a moment the boisterous laughter,
Or the curses that rang o'er the keen autumn air.

Not a sigh, nor an accent of ruth had they for him,
Done to death for their pleasure that ill fated day,
Not a bet was delayed, as the ambulance bore him,
For why should they fret o'er inanimate clay?

'Tis the way of the world, little pity has Fashion
For the innocent cause of its momentary gloom,
Aye! Pity is silent, and none hath compassion
Save the jockey-lad's mother, who weeps o'er his tomb

HIS NAME WAS BILL.

YES! he look'd a thorough Briton, as he ask'd us to afford
    Food and raiment for his young ones, and each member of
      our Board
Felt a tear of manly pity trickle down each bearded cheek
When he wept about his dead boy, buried only yester week.

In response unto our question, as to how he fared so ill,
He inform'd us he was Hinglish, and his Christian name was Bill;
And he spake about his mother, how her agèd, kindly brow
Would receive another wrinkle, could she only see him now.

Had endorsed a note in friendship, hence an alien now must roam ;
Told us in a burst of candour, " Things is different, too, at 'ome."
This we knew, and so we told him ; then we asked him to retire,
Whilst we wrestled with the question : Should we grant him his .
    desire ?

Was he honest and deserving ?   And the Chair rose to its feet
With th₂ comforting assurance that it ne'er had chanced to meet
One whose walk and conversation savoured less of worldly guile
Than this pilgrim at the portal, who had said his name was Bill.

But our board is ultra English: soon the grumblers' notes were
heard,
And our old-time champion kicker said the thing was too absurd ;
And, with brutal, undiluted Anglo-Saxon insolence
Dubb'd the Chairman's *ipse dixit*, " Hunsupported hevidence."

Dark the air with points of order, and sarcastic lightnings flash'd;
Deep our mutter'd " *miserere* " as their moral thunders crash'd ;
But they ceas'd not till exhaustion laved them with perspiring
showers,
And the art vituperative had exhausted all its powers.

Then our Vice rose to the question in a ponderous sort of way ;
He was quite a judge of faces, and he'd only this to say :
If we lack'd an honest workman, we had simply but to call
In the man we'd ask'd to tarry for a season in the hall.

This smooth'd down the opposition, still'd the mutter'd notes of
war,
And we voted meat and groceries to the man outside the door.
Then the Chair and Vice-Chair, who had stood by him thro'
thick and thin,
Stepp'd outside unto that worthy—stepp'd outside to ask him in.

Why, oh ! why that yell of horror from our Chairman's lusty
throat ?
Why the Vice-Chair's howl of anguish, " Where's my Persian
lamb-skin coat ? "
Vanish'd were the spoils of Persia, and, by Jove ! they're absent
still ;
Absent, too, that honest workman, who had said his name was
Bill.

ISAIAH BROWN.

FAIR and pleasant Monte Carlo! by calm Paillon's winding
    shore,
Tender mem'ries linger round thee of the wild, hot days of yore,
When the tones of sweet voiced lovers, and the gentle southern
    breeze
Woo'd the smiles of chic Celestine, or the sighs of Heloise.

I remember, Monte Carlo! standing by thy tapis vert,
And the pilgrims from Beersheba-unto-Dan were gather'd there,
Flinging Naps and five franc pieces, passe and manque, on black
    and red,
Transversale, en plein et carré, and an oftime plunge on Z.

Cocottes from the Quartier Breda, redolent of La Mabille—
English 'Arry " hon a houting," with his plunder'd master's till—
Grandes dames from the statelier faubourgs—swells from Hyde
    Park and the Mall
Chevaliers and Scamperowskis—gather'd in that gambling hell.

Parbleus! shrugs, and fierce sac—r—r—ings, as the Frenchman
    only can,
Faces, flushed with deep excitement, fev'rishly the tables scan,
And the croupiers, pale! impassive! raked their gold into the
    maw
Of dead Blanc's fair, fat and forty, and her princely son-in-law.

But one face, above all others, rivetted my wandering gaze,
Ever present is yon victim of the gambler's madd'ning craze,
On my shuddering heart and hearing rings his wild cry, as he
    tossed,
With a curse, his last Napoleon on the fatal red—and lost.

Nought to me that homely Saxon, clad in loose ill-fitting clothes,
Yet my heart went out unto him, yea ! I longed to hear his woes,

And I follow'd when he vanish'd, heedless of the table's jeer,
More to me his awful anguish than the bloodless gamester's
  sneer.

Swift his pace, but mine was swifter—as he gain'd the alley'd
  way,
I could hear this gibb'ring madman, ruin'd by accursèd play ;
Saw the fateful barrel's gleaming flash athwart his temple—and
God be thanked ! ! an iron grasp had stay'd the suicidal hand.

Suave officials sought to soothe him, begg'd him to assuage his
  ire,
All in vain ! he cried the louder, death was now his sole desire,
What to him were peace or quiet ?   Who could soften his dis-
  tress ?
Far from home, a broken stranger ! ruin'd he, and penniless.

Whisper'd they—the administration might exercise parental
  care,
If Monsieur would but refrain from climbing up the golden stair,
And they show'd this "rosbif booldogue" 'tis not according
  unto Hoyle
Thus, for swells who're "on their uppers," to shuffle off this
  mortal coil.

And, anon, the administration reprehensively did chide,
And it spake in terms abhorrent of that baffled suicide,
God had given it the casino for its own and country's good,
And, m'1 foi ! 'twas most ungrateful thus to stain its halls with
  blood.

But, it said, it hated scandal, and, in short, would compromise,
Would Monsieur accept its offer ?   And—all speechless with sur-
  prise
" Done and done," I heard him twitter, saw him pocket fifty
  pounds,
And that night he left forever fair Monaco's narrow bounds.

Ruin'd? Nay! Would you believe it that those Monte Carlo
  cranks
Subsidized a scamp whose losings hardly totall'd thirty francs?
Poppy-cock they found his ravings, and his pistol well rammed
  down
With note paper, and this on it—" Thank yer, *Gents!* Isaiah
  Brown."

Fare thee well, sweet Monte Carlo, by calm Paillon's winding
  shore,
Golden sunshine rest upon thee, though I ne'er should see thee
  more.
Ta-ta, Vauriens! Scamperowskis! Bye-bye, rooks of London
  town!
Pales your light beneath the glory of that cad—Isaiah Brown.

IN THE WARD OF ST. JOHN THE DIVINE.

BRUIS'D and batter'd I lay till the ambulance came,
    And the arm of the law held a space
Where rough and philanthropist selfishly fought
    For one look at a pallid young face.
Then I fainted away from the torturing pain,
    And consciousness never was mine,
Till I gazed from the sheets of a hospital cot
    In the ward of Saint John the Divine.

What vision was yon—when the doctors had gone,
    That seem'd as an angel of light,
In a frou-frouless gown, and a dainty white cap,
    Who hath ruth on my dolorous plight!
Ah! I would that this pen could the winsomeness trace
    Of that brow, and her nose—aquiline—
And the calm witching grace of my dignified nurse
    In the ward of Saint John the Divine.

Believe me! 'twas tempting to have those red lips
  (As Pat says) "adjacently close,"
And pleasant to gaze on those deft little hands
  As they portion'd the nauseous dose;
And her soft, low, "good night"—when the long shadows fell,
  Touch'd my heart so, I ne'er could repine
At the pain and the ache of the weary night hours
  In the ward of Saint John the Divine.

But the pain and the ache of those weary night hours
  Seem'd as naught when the morning-light came,
And brought in its wake—to replace the night-watch,
  "Sister Alice," (and sweet as her name).
Oh how soft was her touch, and delightfully cool!
  Yet, to flirting she ne'er would incline,
Demurely she said that the word was unknown
  In the ward of Saint John the Divine.

By the blood of my sires! Could those violet eyes,
  Never a lover's hot pulses have stirr'd?   .
Had no answering flush ever mantled that brow
  When the acents of passion were heard?
So I flung down my glove in the lists of true love,
  Where suff'ring had long held her shrine,
How the Board would have stared had it known of such work
  In the ward of Saint John the Divine!

But the castle held out, and its fair chatelaine
  Smil'd unconscious of Love's potent spell,
And oft, when I deemed that the fortress was won,
  I had failed at the first parallel.
Yet who—save a dastard—would count a repulse
  As defeat, and, despairing, resign
One jot of his claim to the loveliest form
  In the ward of Saint John the Divine?

'Tis true she rebuked; but I also was heard,
  And reproof grew suspiciously less,
Till, one day, her reply to a question I asked
  Had muchly the flavour of " yes."
As the Board went no further than brotherly love,
  " Sister Alice " was ask'd to resign,
And each pillow was wet with the tear of regret
  In the ward of Saint John the Divine.

When the north wind is high, and the curtains are drawn,
  In the firelight's calm, ruddy glow,
I sit, and I dream of the hours that are fled
  To the shades of the dear long ago ;
And the maiden who fills my post-prandial pipe,
  And whose cheek nestles close unto mine,
Is the image of her who enraptured my heart
  In the ward of Saint John the Divine.

THE CYCLONE.

THE cyclone's an agitator,
    And a special ventilator,
That works the bailiwick for all its worth.
    Oh, the sweet voluptuous ease
    Of its calmly go-as-you-please,
As it mixes up the objects of its mirth.

    And when its sighs are over—
    When the natives creep from cover
And gaze with sadness o'er the festive scene,
    They know its gentle zephyrs
    Have worked their best endeavours,
And left the land-marks few and far between.

THE DENTIST'S CHAIR.

ᚶOND the portals of woe stands that ill-fated chair ;
   And the demon of torture holds revelry there.
Sad pilgrims have sought it—distracted with pain—
And, finding, have sneaked from the purlieus again.
I hate it like poison—oh ! blest if I don't !
And my *bete noir's* the wretch who was smilingly wont,
With a purr that was feline, to inveigle me there
And play Hamlet with me in that plush-covered chair.

Oh ! the ways of that fiend are chuck full of guile.
Surely blandness itself is as nought to his smile
When he told me he plainly detected the thrall
Of decay on my molars, incisors, *et al.*,
The filling of which would be free from all pain—
So free I should wish it done over again.
Reassured, I sat down with a half-muttered prayer,
And the circus began in that plush-covered chair.

All the neighbours for blocks heard a scalp-lifting yell;
And the language in which I endeavoured to tell
To humanity's ear of the jab which he gave
At the nerve of the " canine " I'd striven to save,
And the leer of the wretch—when another loud roar
Told the public a Trust had been shattered once more—
As he asked me—vulgarian !—to " keep on my hair "
And be seated once more in that plush-covered chair.

As clay in the hands of the potter, forsooth !
I sat whilst he quarried a hole in the tooth,
And, without my consent, introduced to the scene
A treadle which worked like a sewing machine—
Whir-r ! Fiz !! Snip !!!—Hold ! Enough !—Oh ! my agon-
   ized shouts,

As I ask'd for my head or its last whereabouts ;
But he only vouchsafed an inimical glare
As he pinion'd me down in that plush-covered chair.

Low insult to injury was piled on me when
He tweak'd the snub nose of the saddest of men.
Then up into space that ineffable scamp
(After toasting his gold at a small spirit lamp)
Pegg'd and hammer'd away with soul-harrowing blows
Till, wrought up to madness, I wildly arose,
Seiz'd my hat, gloves and cane, yes! and fled in despair
From the awful embrace of that plush-covered chair.

Sing of Cæsar's great heart! of the Twelfth Legion braves !
Let your tears dew the green of Thermopylæ's graves !
Laud the mashers who swam through the corpse-choking fosse,
As the Crescent light paled in the glare of the Cross !
Weave your garlands of praise for the stout-hearted blades
Who kick'd up their heels in the glorious Crusades !
Tell of Bayard, du Guesclin and Ralph Bras de Fer !
Yet the whole of these heroes, who lived but to dare
Would have bolted like fun from that plush-covered chair.

VANITY FAIR.

'Tis the height of the season, and matron and maid
 Are met at Society's call,
From eighteen to forty, or more in the shade,
 They are crying their wares from each stall ;
And the downy-lipp'd youth with the feminine bang
 And the hoary-browed roué are there,
As the summer wind echoes the din and the clang
 Of the hucksters at Vanity Fair.

And what is thy guerdon, O, Vanity Fair
    (For on this I would fain hear the truth)?
Of the kisses of Love, dost thou offer a share
    To honest, though dowerless, youth?
May virtue and worth, in those fair halls of thine,
    Hold their own with the ag'd millionaire?
Can the heart of true love ever rear its fair shrine
    At the altar of Vanity Fair?

" A fig for true lovers," quoths Vanity Fair,
    " Here maidens are bought and are sold,
Regardless of worth or of youth's golden hair,
    To the purse that is heaviest with gold."
Then farewell to peace—to the happy fireside—
    And hopeless the heart-broken prayer
For the blessings of home, whilst fond love is denied
    At the weddings of Vanity Fair.

" NINETY-EIGHT."

" **F**REE! 'Ninety-eight'! yer free again," Jackson, the warder,
    said,
And " 98 " went forth once more—a living man, yet dead.

Dead to the world, dead to the past, long agonizing years
Within yon hateful walls had well nigh dried the fount of tears.

Long, long ago,—one night,—when wine and wassail usher'd
    strife
His arm of ire had stained the altar in the House of Life.

A kindly record blasted by one madd'ning blow,—but he
Had borne his discipline, and now they told him he was—free!

Free! oh what mockery it seem'd! Free! whither could he go?
Dead! kith and kin,—save one, and she unwitting of his woe.

She, to far distant scenes removed, had lisp'd a father's name,
And grown to glorious womanhood, unconscious of his shame.

To easier, brighter paths of sin, the tempter's voice beguiled,
But " Ninety-eight " had will'd his choice—to see once more his
child.

To clasp her in his arms again—the thought itself was bliss,
And press upon her pure young brow, a father's sinless kiss.

And, at life's close, her own dear hands would tend his dying bed,
And do those last sad offices Love renders to its dead.

His *child!* and at that sacred name, fast fell the blinding tears,
The first those poor old faded eyes had known through grievous
years.

Oh Heaven-sent tears that bless poor bruisèd hearts, as summer
rain,
Descending on the parchèd earth, revives the drooping grain.

Distant the goal, his pathway one of thorns, that bruis'd and tore
Him, struggling on, Despair behind, Hope beck'ning on before.

The farmer's hind view'd him askance (his ill dissembled ire
Saw visions rise of plunder'd roosts and garner'd stores afire).

The passing wain's rude waggoner threaten'd his circling thong,
When Misery sought of Insolence to make the way less long.

The village mother closer clasp'd her helpless little trust
When Famine at the portal stood, and begg'd a simple crust.

But the poor wand'rer's gentle words unbent each harden'd brow,
For " Ninety-eight's " bruised, way-worn heart, was very patient
now.

His wayside couch knew him no more when scorching day was
    done,
His fellow-traveller the moon, his curfew-bell, the sun.

His brother tramp's sarcastic cry hung heavy o'er the breeze,
Unkenn'd by one whose onward march had scorn of leisured ease.

How could he cry a halt, when ev'ry step brought him more near
To the fair Mecca of his heart,—to the Hope he held most dear ?

And no man guess'd the happy dreams that guil'd his onward way,
Of parting lost in union, as the shadow'd hour in day.

As the impatient reader flings aside the halting page,
So in such hours he flung from him the lingering steps of Age.

And, for a season, youth was his, and Fancy's loom did weave
A future blest for him and his, where none should vex, nor grieve.

Yea ! she should walk in silk attire, and the spoils of many lands
Would yield glad tribute to her charms, and deck her dainty
    hands.

Days wax'd to weeks, and weeks to months, ere distance knew
    control,
And the toil-worn feet of " Ninety-eight " had reached their
    journey's goal.

And thus it chanced, one winter's night, the wand'rer stood before
Her lattice pane, and, unseen, gazed upon his child once more.

How beautiful she seem'd, so like another, long since dead
(She who had won his manhood's love, ere Youth and Honour
    fled).

But not alone ! for " Ninety-eight " could see and almost hear
One, by her side, who spake of love to her both held so dear.

What mortal sleeper has not known the bitter waking pain
From pleasant visions of the night, to cold, grey morn again ?

So, by yon glance, the white-haired watcher knew these youthful
    lives
Were not for him, the leper, redolent of gaol and gyves.

What place had he, a branded man, in such a scene as this?
Can the lost spirits doom'd from hope, dwell in the realms of bliss?

How *could* he blast this fair young life, *he*—with his tarnish'd
    fame?
What could his coming lend to her, save the bitter sense of shame?

Ah! *now* he knew his treasured dream had faded from his sight,
As the last beam of eve is lost in shadows of the night.

Though filial love be beautiful, though filial love should last,
Come weal! come woe! *she* should not share, nor know his dark-
    ened past.

And with one stricken cry that demons might have wept to hear,
The outcast pass'd into the night from the hope he held most dear.

Like some poor wounded animal the homeless wand'rer crept
For shelter 'neath a fallen tree, whilst the whole village slept.

(Oh ye! safe in your haven-homes, where the tempter woos in
    vain,
Have ye no tears for this poor heart, curs'd with the brand of
    Cain!)

When peacefully the morrow dawned—the morrow of that night—
Lo! Heaven had cloth'd the landscape in a garb of spotless white.

And 'neath its canopy lay one whose soul had pass'd away
From the dark night of tears and woe, to the light of endless day.

For in that hour of early morn, men call "the Hour of Fate"—
His pilgrimage was done. Safe with his God was "Ninety-eight."